MW00639704

Climbing
Guide
2nd Edition

By Garth Bruce

Disclaimer
The activities described in this book are potentially dangerous and can result in severe injury or death. The information in this book may be inaccurate and you are fully responsible for all personal injury while approaching or climbing the routes described in this book. Weather conditions in the areas described in this book change continually which can result in dangerous climbing conditions. All the potential hazards are too numerous to list here. If you do not have adequate climbing knowledge and experience, hire a qualified professional instructor. You assume full responsibility or liability when using this guide.

Exit 38 Rock Climbing Guide

Cover Photo

Danette Boka on "Winter Rushing In" (p.73), 5.8. Photo by Laura Morton, photographer for Seattle Times Newspaper. All other photos and quotes by Garth Bruce unless otherwise stated.

Published and Distributed by

Free Solo Publishing
FreeSoloPublishing@NorthBendRock.com

ISBN: 0-9723708-3-8

Table of Contents

Introduction

In November of 2001, when the world was a lot quieter, the "Exit 38 Rock Climbing Guide" book was published. It detailed three climbing areas in the Exit 38 area; Mt Washington, Deception Crags, and the Far Side. In these three areas there are 20 separate climbing walls and over 200 routes.

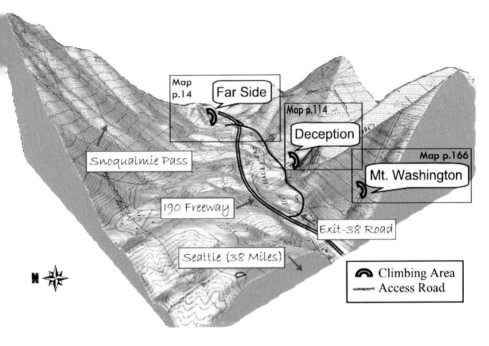

Over the last few years, the Exit 38 climbing area has become the most popular rock climbing area in western Washington. The most notable reasons for its popularity include proximity to Seattle, well marked trails, hundreds of routes, scenic views, and some of the best rock climbing in the state.

The three climbing areas at Exit 38 (Mt. Washington, Deception, and Far Side) are about a mile apart from each other. Because there are a considerable number of climbs at each area, and given the hiking time to reach the routes, most climbers will only climb in one area in a given day.

Introduction

The climbing walls are listed in the book from closest to furthest hiking distance from the parking lot. The first wall listed in an area is the first wall you will reach from the parking area. The last wall listed is the furthest from the parking area.

Very few routes have been added at the Mt Washington and Deception area. At the Far Side, however, there has been a lot of activity, hence one of the main reasons for this book.

Five new walls with over forty routes have been added to the Far Side collection, giving it the greatest number of routes in the Exit 38 area. Most of the new routes are on existing climbing walls, the exception being in a completely new wall that was developed in 2005 called Neverland.

The Far Side still has a lot of potential for new routes. So, expect many more great routes, and feel free to trash this book given you'll most likely be buying another updated climbing book around 2009.

Several changes have been made to the revised edition of this book. In fact, most of the book has been rewritten from the original. One element of the book that is unchanged from the first edition is the multitude of pictures. The book includes pictures of the parking areas, trails, every route, and even the toilets.

The first thing you'll notice, hopefully, about the new edition is that it's all color. Color adds a lot of information to the route images, trails, turn offs, and area features. It also adds a bit to the cost of publishing the book but since you're reading this you obviously could afford it.

Several other key features have been added to the new revision. They include new routes, enhanced trail maps, wall overview photos with routes, and even climbing itineraries. All of this adds up to what I hope is a better way to navigate the area and find the routes you want to climb.

Introduction

If going vertical is new to you then continue reading the introduction. It will help you with common terminology and symbol explanations. If you've got the climbing lingo, fast forward to the statistics summary on pages 15 (Far Side), 116 (Deception), or 167 (Mt Washington) to pick the area that best matches your climbing ability and hiking time requirements.

Next, find a computer connected to the internet and surf to www.northbendrock.com. It provides the latest information about the climbing areas (including the Exit 32 climbing area) and also includes very useful panoramic images of the parking areas, trails, and walls which will help visually familiarize you with the areas and minimize your wandering.

If you're just visiting the area, and don't have a lot of extra time, check out the climbing itineraries starting on page 109 (Far Side), 161 (Deception), or 241 (Mt Washington). Each itinerary gives easy to follow, step-by-step instructions for accessing climbing great beginning, intermediate, and advanced routes in the shortest period of time. Only interested in bagging the best routes? If so, then page 108 (Far Side), 160 (Deception), or 240 (Mt Washington) has what you need.

One thing not in the book is route beta. Beta can be very useful for longer alpine routes, but in the sport climbing world beta is mostly for entertainment. Also, every climber is different. Good beta for one climber is not so good for the next. For these reasons, and to keep the books cost at a minimum, route beta has been moved to the web at www.northbendrock.com/routes/beta.

Note: This book is NOT designed to be a "How To" Climbing guide. It will not tell you how to climb safely or what equipment you should or shouldn't use. If you're not sure about any of these points then hire a climbing guide or take a class at your local indoor climbing gym. Also, make sure you get your mother's permission.

Introduction

Mt Washington

- Best parking area
- 15-65 minute hike from parking lot
- Series of walls along the Mt. Washington trail
- Best views in the valley
- Less crowded than Deception Crags area
- No multi pitch routes, four traditional (trad i.e. gear) routes
- 20% of the routes can be top roped (more than other areas)
- Best Beginner wall, "Peannacle"; Intermediate wall, "Amazonia"; Advanced wall, "Lost Resort"
- Lower walls shaded, upper walls sunny

Deception

- 5-15 minute hike from parking lot
- Good selection of beginning routes
- Scenic views of the freeway
- Great trails to all walls
- One multi-pitch route, no traditional (gear) routes
- Best Beginner wall, "Write-Off"; Intermediate wall "We Did Rock"; Advanced wall, "Nevermind"
- Toilets close to the climbing walls
- Most popular (because of quick and easy access)
- Usually free of snow and climbable in the winter

Far Side

- Most Routes
- Several excellent multi pitch routes
- Good selection of beginner to advanced climbs
- 5-50 minute hike from parking area
- No potties
- Several multi-pitch routes, one gear route
- Best Beginner wall, "Gritscone"; Intermediate wall, "Interstate Park"; Advanced wall, "Overhaul"
- Easy access to a nice beach on the Snoqualmie River
- Sunniest routes i.e. great climbing in the spring and fall

Introduction

Getting To Exit-38

If you've never used a brain bucket (helmet) climbing then you may not have yet realized that "Exit 38" is the actual name of the Exit that you take off of Interstate 90. To reach the Exit 38 climbing area, drive east on Interstate 90 (I-90), 37.3 miles (8 miles east of North Bend) and take a right off the Exit 38 exit. The exit is about a 35 minute drive from Seattle or a 5 minute drive from North Bend. For more detail and specific directions from your location, check an online internet map, for example www.expedia.com/maps.

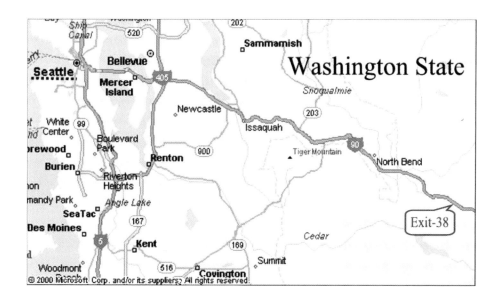

One thing to note, Exit 38 is actually a long side road next to I-90 with an on/off ramp at each end. The west bound on/off ramp is by the Mt Washington climbing area. The east bound on/off ramp is 2 miles up the side road by the Far Side Climbing area. If this made absolutely no sense, try the visual on page 5.

Route Difficulty

Route difficulty ratings in this book are based on the YDS System. If you think YDS stands for "Yellow Does Stain" then you might want to reconsider rock climbing. Just in case you can't get your money back for this book, here's a summary of the YDS rating system.

YDS (Yosemite Decimal System) is broken into 5 classes ranging from flat lander areas (Class 1) to technical rock climbing where a safety rope is required (Class 5). Class 5 is further divided into several sub categories ranging from 5.0 (lots of holds for hand and feet) to 5.15 (no holds for you hands or feet and its overhanging).

5.5 thru 5.7 is generally, in sport climbing, considered beginning level. 5.8 thru 5.10 is intermediate, 5.11 thru 5.13 is advanced. 5.14 thru 5.15 are for an elite few.

The graph below shows the route difficulty of each of the areas. For example, if you're an advanced climber (5.11+), then the Mt Washington area will have more for you. If you're just getting started (5.6+) then the Far Side would be a good destination choice.

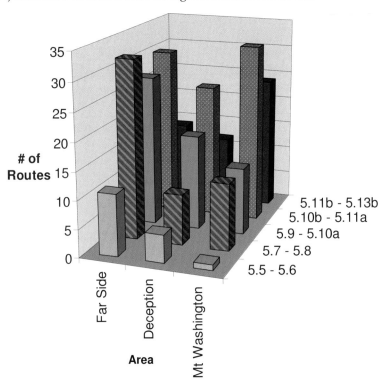

Symbol Definitions

There are three places in the book where you will find strange symbols: on the Wall Maps (simple topos), Route Tables, and Route Pictures.

Wall Maps

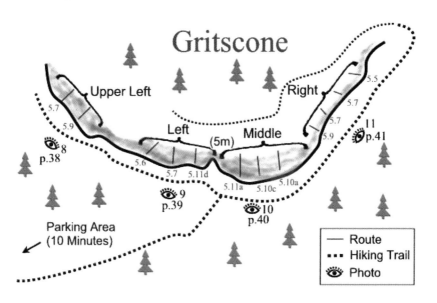

Each climbing wall has a simple topo map. The purpose of the map is to outline how the wall is laid out with respect to the hiking trails, routes, and pictures.

In the Gritscone example above, the wall is divided into four sections; Upper Left, Left, Middle, and Right. Each section has a corresponding photo showing all the routes. Each wall will also have the height listed in meters, **(5m)** or 5 meters high in the example above.

A dashed line (---) indicates the hiking trail. Red lines (**|**) show the location of a route. Below is the route difficulty rating (**5.7**).

The photo location icon (👁) shows where the photo was taken, with respect to the wall, and lists the picture number (**9**). Below that is the page number for the route photo (**p.39**).

Symbol Definitions

Route Tables

Route tables provide a summary of the routes. They are intended to give you a quick reference for just the information you need. Here's a typical example:

Difficulty	Route	Bolts	Rating	Name
5.10a ↻	C	7	★ ★ ★	Heaven Can Wait
5.11b	D	26 (Pro to 9")	★	Diaper on, Climb on! ❗ See #21 p.102

Difficulty: Yosemite Decimal System number. An "estimate" of the effort needed to reach the top. The arrow symbol "↻" next to the rating means the routes can be safely top roped.

Route: Letter used to identify the specific route in the photo. Listed in ascending order, from left to right.

Bolts: Number of bolts on the route, not including the anchor. If additional protection (Pro) is required it is listed in parenthesis with the largest piece needed.

Rating: 1 to 4 stars. Route fun factor; 4 stars being the best, 1 star the worst.

    ★ ★ ★ ★   Do whatever it takes to get on the route
    ★ ★ ★   A good, rewarding route that will enrich your life.
    ★ ★   Imagine it's a 4 star route
    ★   Friends don't let friends climb these routes

Name: The name given by the person who created the route. A bold exclamation point (❗) means there is potential danger and you should read the note in the Route Warning table on the page listed before climbing the route.

Symbol Definitions

Route Photographs

Every route listed in this book has an associated photo. Most of the photos will show two or more routes. Because of the lens distortion, time of day, condition of the rock, condition of the photographer, and so forth, the picture may look slightly different from what you see.

Below is a typical photo, which has three symbols:

 : Yosemite Decimal System (YDS) route difficulty rating followed by a letter to identify the route.

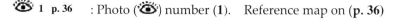 : Approximate route path you might follow if you want to reach the anchors and avoid the big whipper.

 : Anchors at the top of the route, usually two sections of chain.

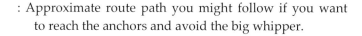 : Photo (👁) number (**1**).   Reference map on (**p. 36**)

Far Side

There are seven separate climbing areas at Far Side; Overhaul, Gritscone, Gun Show, Interstate Park, Easy Street, Winter Block, and Neverland. Each area has the classical Exit 38 style - big, bold, and beautiful holds which provide for a broad range of climbing entertainment.

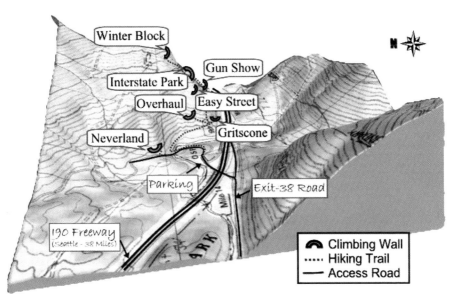

Gritscone, Easy Street, and Interstate Park have the easiest routes, Neverland and Gunshow have a good range of intermediate routes, and Overhaul has the most difficult routes, requiring additional stimulants and/or steroids.

The Far Side has a lot of things going for it; great climbs, sunny exposure, beaches, nude sun bathing, and even bird houses. One thing that it doesn't have (girls pay attention) is a place to potty in private. So if you're the modest type, then don't drink or eat anything the day before you go climbing and you should be okay.

Unfortunately, there has been some route vandalism at the Far Side, mostly consisting of chopped bolts and stolen hangers. So, carry extra draws, check www.northbendrock.com web site for route updates, and report any damage to the routes by sending email to info@northbendrock.com.

Area Summary

Everything you need to know, and a lot you didn't need to know about the area, is nicely formatted in the following table:

Area	Height (Meters)	# of Routes	Hiking Time (Minutes)	Elev. Gain (Feet)
Neverland	15 - 70	17	8	165
Gritscone	10	11	10	200
Gun Show	40	10	18	450
Easy Street	35	3	15	503
Overhaul	20	29	15	704
Interstate Park	10 - 20	31	23	515
Winter Block	15	4	28	1043

Elevation Profile

The elevation profile graph shows you how much elevation you gain and how far the hike is from the parking area to reach a climbing wall. As shown in the graph below, Neverland requires the least about of perspiration to reach, Winter Block the most.

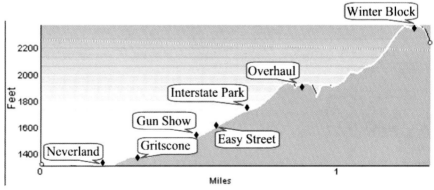

If you're coming from the Seattle area (eastbound), turn right at the bottom of the Exit-38 off-ramp and follow the paved road for 2 miles. The parking area is 100 meters past the Interstate 90 overpass.

If you're coming from Snoqualmie pass (westbound), turn right at the bottom of the Exit-38 off-ramp and the parking area is 100 meters on the left.

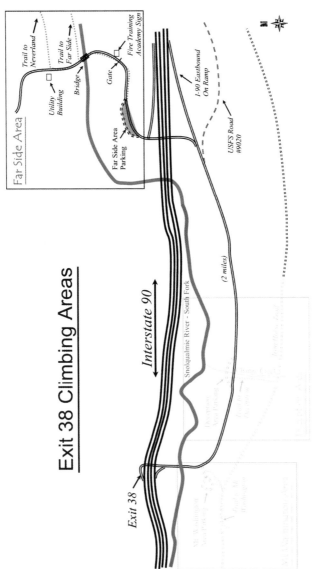

Parking at Far Side

Unlike the luxurious Mt Washington climbing area, Far Side simply offers a place to pull off the road. The good news is it's near a high voltage power line which does a fantastic job of reducing the bug population in the summer time.

From the parking area, hike 4 minutes on the paved State Fire Training road until you reach a bridge over the Snoqualmie River. The main hiking trail starts just after you cross the bridge on the right side. The Neverland wall trail is 100m further up the road on the right.

Overhaul Wall was one of the first walls developed at the Far Side. It is a long wall divided into three climbing sections; Relief Camp, Motherland, and Slabbage Patch.

The lower portion of the wall, Relief Camp, has mostly 5.10a – 5.11a routes on a slightly inverted face. It has the unique characteristic of being half shade (in the trees) and half sun (above the trees). The middle section, Motherland, offers a wide range of climbing difficulty. It receives the most sun and is a great place for early spring and fall climbing. If you're just getting into the sport of rock climbing, then the upper portion of the wall, Slabbage Patch, offers several excellent 5.7-5.9 level routes.

Overhaul

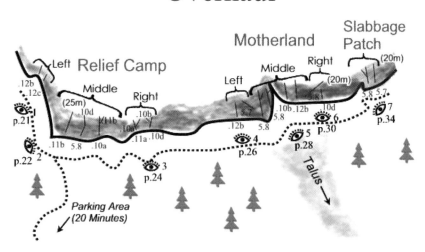

Getting to Overhaul

To reach Overhaul wall, hike down the paved road from the parking area to the main climbing trail (p.17) Turn right, just past the bridge, and hike up the main trail for 5 minutes (.3 miles) to a junction.

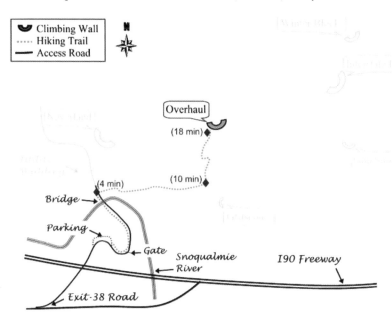

At the junction, take the trail to the left (the right side trail leads to Gritscone & upper walls). Continue on this trail for another 7 minutes (.4 miles) to the lower left section of Overhaul.

GPS Coord. for trail junction: N 47.25.84 by W 121.37.37

👁 1 p. 18

Difficulty	Route	Bolts	Rating	Name
5.12b	A	5	★	Ghost
5.12c	B	6	★	Green Lantern

☐ Ghost _____ Date _____

☐ Green Lantern _____ Date _____

Left - Josh, Red Lining the rap, on
"Kiss Of The Crowbar" - 5.7 (p.70)

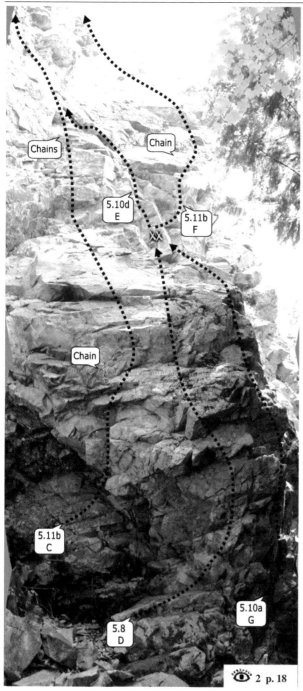

Relief Camp - Middle

Difficulty	Route	Bolts	Rating	Name
5.11b	C	9	★★	Complete Overhaul
5.8	D	3	★★	Chain Gain
5.10d	E	10	★★★	Mr. Fixit
5.11b	F	10	★★★	Chain Gang
5.10a	G	4	★★	Shelf Serve

☐ Complete Overhaul _____

_____

_____

_____ Date _____

☐ Chain Gain _____

_____

_____ Date _____

☐ Mr. Fixit _____

_____

_____ Date _____

☐ Chain Gang _____

_____

_____ Date _____

☐ Shelf Serve_____

_____

_____ Date _____

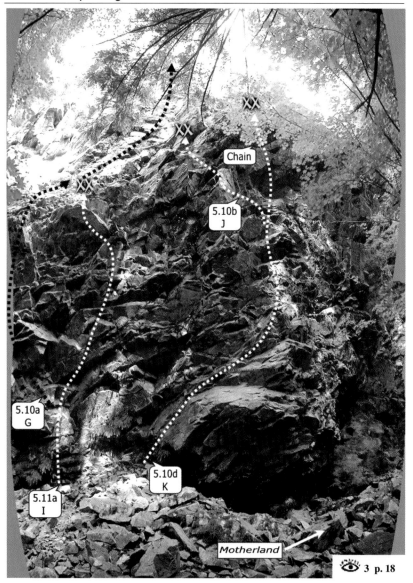

Chain

5.10b
J

5.10a
G

5.10d
K

5.11a
I

Motherland

3 p. 18

Relief Camp – Right

Difficulty	Route	Bolts	Rating	Name
5.10a	G	11	★★★	Rhino Relief
5.11a ↻	I	0	★★★	Give Until It Hurts
5.10b	J	6	★	Controlled Bleeding
5.10d	K	6	★★★	Jugular Vein

☐ Rhino Relief _____

_____

_____ Date _____

☐ Give Until It Hurts _____

_____

_____ Date _____

☐ Controlled Bleeding _____

_____

_____ Date _____

☐ Jugular Vein _____

_____

_____ Date _____

Relief Camp

Slabbage Patch

4 p. 18

Difficulty	Route	Bolts	Rating	Name
5.12b	A	4	★	Flubber
5.7	B	4	★★	False Pretenses ❗ See #1 p. 106

☐ Flubber _____ Date _____

☐ False Pretenses _____ Date _____

Right - Wayne, feeling the sketch, on "Absolutely Nothing" – 5.9 (p.152)

Motherland - Middle

Far Side

Difficulty	Route	Bolts	Rating	Name
5.7	B	4	★★	False Pretenses
5.8	C	4	★★	Cornery Bypass
5.8	D	4	★★	Corner's Inquest
5.10a	E	6	★★	Toying With My Affections
5.10a	F	7	★★	Toying With My Afflictions
5.11a	G	7	★★	Foreplay
5.10b	H	7	★★★	Sheltered Upbringing

☐ False Pretenses _____

_____ Date _____

☐ Cornery Bypass _____

_____ Date _____

☐ Corner's Inquest _____

_____ Date _____

☐ Toying With My Affections _____

_____ Date _____

☐ Toying With My Afflictions _____

_____ Date _____

☐ Foreplay _____ _____

_____ Date _____

☐ Sheltered Upbringing _____ _____

_____ Date _____

Far Side - 29

Motherland – Middle

Far Side

5 p. 18

Difficulty	Route	Bolts	Rating	Name
5.10b	H	7	★★★	Sheltered Upbringing
5.11a	I	9	★★★	Moreplay ! See #2 p.106
5.12b	J	6	★★★	Hovering Mother
5.12a	K	6	★★★	Offspring
5.8	L	8	★★	On The Outskirts ! See #3 p.106

☐ Sheltered Upbringing _____

_____

_____ Date _____

☐ Moreplay _____

_____

_____ Date _____

☐ Hovering Mother _____

_____

_____ Date _____

☐ Offspring _____

_____

_____ Date _____

☐ On The Outskirts _____

_____

_____ Date _____

5.8
L

5.10d
M

👁 6 p. 18

Slabbage Patch

Difficulty	Route	Bolts	Rating	Name
5.8	L	7	★★	On the Outskirts ❗See #3 p.106
5.10d	M	3	★★	Stretcher Case

Right – Collen and daughter Meg enjoying the afternoon on "Pete's Possum Palace" – 5.7 (p.41)

Slabbage Patch

Difficulty	Route	Bolts	Rating	Name	
5.9	A	13	★★	End Run	! See #4 p.106
5.9	C	7	★★★	Siamese Dream	
5.9	D	4	★	Nature Boy	
5.7	E	5	★★	Party Girl	

☐ End Run _____

_____

_____

_____ Date _____

☐ Siamese Dream _____

_____

_____

_____ Date _____

☐ Nature Boy _____

_____

_____

_____ Date _____

☐ Party Girl _____

_____

_____

_____ Date _____

Gritscone

Gritscone is little crag, more like a large boulder, which was most likely exposed and scrubbed clean during the last ice age about 12,000 years ago. If you're just learning how to rock climb this is a great place to visit. The routes are short (four bolts or less), easily top roped, and mostly between 5.5 - 5.9.

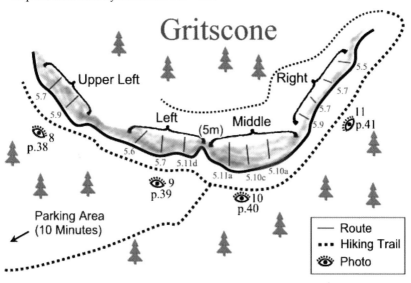

The upper left portion of the rock has a uniquely course texture which makes for some interesting slab climbing and, if you're not careful, quick skin removal. The left section is steeper but with big, reassuring hand holds. The middle section is slightly overhanging with the most difficult route (5.11d) on the rock. The right side offers several short beginning level routes.

Words of Wisdom

To love someone is to learn the song of their heart and to sing it to them when they have forgotten it. -Anonymous

To reach Gritscone wall, hike down the paved road from the parking area to the main climbing trail (p.17) Turn right, just past the bridge, and hike up the main trail for 5 minutes (.3 miles) to a junction.

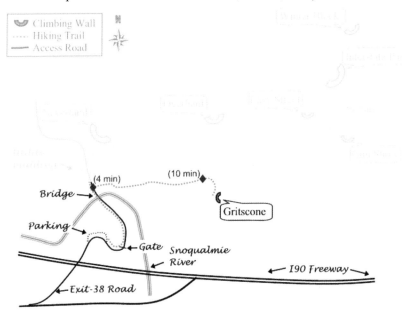

Turn right at the junction (left trail goes to Overhaul) 10 meters, across a wet area, and to another trail fork. Take the right trail (left trail continues on to Gun Show and Interstate Park). Follow it for 60 meters to the lower left section of the wall.

GPS Coord. for trail junction: N 47.25.83 by W 121.37.37

👁 8 p. 36

Difficulty	Route	Bolts	Rating	Name
5.7	A	3	★★	Needle Magnet
5.9	B	2	★★	Magnetic Anomaly

☐ Needle Magnet _____

_____

_____

_____ Date _____

☐ Magnetic Anomaly _____

_____

_____

_____ Date _____

Difficulty	Route	Bolts	Rating	Name
5.6 ↻	C	3	★★	Lucky Arms
5.7 ↻	D	2	★★	Snaffle Baffler
5.11d	E	3	★	Rough Cut

☐ Lucky Arms _____

_____ Date _____

☐ Snaffle Baffler _____

_____ Date _____

☐ Rough Cut _____

_____ Date _____

10 p. 36

Difficulty	Route	Bolts	Rating	Name
5.11d	E	3	★	Rough Cut
5.11a ↻	F	3	★★	A Girl's Best Friend
5.10c ↻	G	3	★★	Booty Squirrel
5.10a ↻	H	4	★★★	Chica Rapida

☐ Rough Cut _____

_____ Date _____

☐ A Girl's Best Friend _____

_____ Date _____

☐ Booty Squirrel_____

_____ Date _____

☐ Booty Squirrel_____

_____ Date _____

11 p. 36

Difficulty	Route	Bolts	Rating	Name
5.9	I	3	★★★	99 Grit
5.7 ↻	J	3	★★	Pete's Possum Palace
5.7 ↻	K	2	★★	So Funny I Forgot To Rope Up
5.5 ↻	L	2	★★	So Easy I Forgot To Laugh

☐ 99 Grit _____

_____ Date _____

☐ Pete's Possum Palace _____

_____ Date _____

☐ So Funny I Forgot To Rope Up _____

_____ Date _____

☐ So Easy I Forgot To Laugh _____

_____ Date _____

Gun Show

Far Side

Gun Show is a large band of rock below Interstate Park. It got its name from the shooting gallery across Interstate 90. In 2005, the state department barricaded several of the gun party pullouts and posted a "no more needless killing of cans and various other targets" sign. So, unfortunately, the extra excitement you used to get while climbing with live gun fire is now gone and the Gun Show wall needs a new name.

Although the shooting gallery was moved, the freeway wasn't. To say that another way... "IT'S CLOSE TO A MAJOR FREEWAY!" In case you didn't get that it's noisy. So, figure out how you're going to communicate with your partner **before** they start to climb *(can you say "radios?")*.

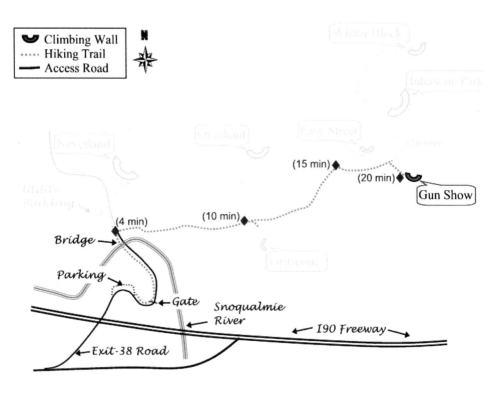

Map legend: Climbing Wall, Hiking Trail, Access Road. N (compass). Locations: Gun Show (20 min), (15 min), (10 min), (4 min), Bridge, Parking, Gate, Snoqualmie River, I90 Freeway, Exit-38 Road.

The wall is still under development so be sure to check www.northbendrock.com periodically for route update information.

To reach Gun Show, hike past the side trail to Gritscone (p.37) 5 minutes and turn to the right. (left trail goes to Winter Block)

GPS Coord:
N 47.25.80
W 121.37.40

Follow this trail for 5 minutes to large log suspended over the trail. Step over the log and hike down the trail for 5 minutes to the base of the Gun Show wall. If you go straight at the log you end up at Headlight Point, which is the bottom left side of Interstate Park.

GPS Coordinate:
N 47.25.80
W 121.37.32

XX XX

5.8
A

5.8
B

👁 12 p. 43

Difficulty	Route	Bolts	Rating	Name
5.8	A	4	★	GS-1
5.8	B	7	★	GS-2

☐ GS-1 _____ Date _____

☐ GS-2 _____ Date _____

5.8
C

👁 13 p. 43

Difficulty	Route	Bolts	Rating	Name	
5.8	C	6	★ ★	GS-3	❗ See #17 p.107

GS-3 _____ Date _____

Gun Show

Far Side

14 p. 43

Difficulty	Route	Bolts	Rating	Name	
5.10b	D	7	★★	GS-4	! See #13 p.107
5.10c	E	4	★★	GS-5	
5.8	F	7	★★	GS-6	! See #18 p.107

☐ GS-4_____ Date _____

☐ GS-5_____ Date _____

☐ GS-6_____ Date _____

5.9
G

👁 15 p. 43

Difficulty	Route	Bolts	Rating	Name
5.9	G	16	★★★	Elation At The End Of Eternity (2 Pitches) ❗ See #9 p.106

☐ Elation At The End Of Eternity _____ Date _____

Difficulty	Route	Bolts	Rating	Name
5.9	H	7	★★	GS-7
5.10a	I	16	★★★	Endless Bliss ❗ See #11 p.106
5.10d	J	4	★	Super Squish
5.11d	K	4	★	GS-8

☐ GS-7 _____ Date _____

☐ Endless Bliss _____ _____ Date _____

☐ Super Squish _____ Date _____

☐ GS-8 _____ Date _____

Gun Show

5.11c
M

5.10c
L

👁 17 p.43

Difficulty	Route	Bolts	Rating	Name
5.10c	L	11	★★	GS-9
5.11c	M	9	★★	GS-10

☐ GS-9 _____ Date _____

☐ GS-10 _____ Date _____

Gun Show

👁 18 p.43

Difficulty	Route	Bolts	Rating	Name
5.10a	N	9	★★★	Web Slinger (1st Pitch)
5.10d	O	9	★★	Web Slinger (2nd Pitch) ❗ See #10 p.106

☐ Web Slinger (1st Pitch) _____ Date _____

_____

_____

☐ Web Slinger (2nd Pitch) _____ Date _____

_____

_____

Interstate Park

Far Side

Interstate Park is a band of rock 20 meters high and 150 meters wide just to the North of the I-90 freeway. Most of the routes are in the 5.7-5.10 difficulty range so it's a great place for intermediate level sport climbers to feel the joy of adrenaline. Also, because of its southern expose, it enjoys lots of year-round sun, which makes it ideal for spring and fall climbing as well as nude sun bathing.

Interstate Park has five walls; Headlight Point, Eastern Block, Squishy Bell, Off-Ramp, and Mayberry. The first three are part of the main upper wall; the second two are below it. These walls now comprise the majority of routes at the Far Side area.

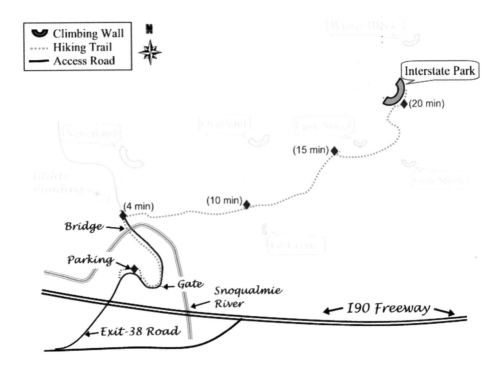

(10m)

Squishy
Bell p. 72

Winter
Block

Off-Ramp p.74

(20m)

Eastern Block p. 62

(15m)

Mayberry p.80

(15m)

Headlight
Point p. 55

Gun Show

(15m)

To reach Interstate Park, hike up the main trail 15 minutes (7 minutes past Gritscone turnoff p. 36) to a side trail on the right. Follow it for 7 minutes down the ridge. *GPS Coordinate: N 47.25.83 by W 121.37.39*

7 minutes after taking a right off of the main trail you'll see the turn off to Gun Show. Continue straight and hike up the ridge another 7 minutes to a small clearing overlooking Interstate 90. This is the bottom of the Headlight Point section of Interstate Park.

GPS Coordinate:
N 47.25.80
W 121.37.32

Headlight point is the left, southern most, section of the Interstate Park area. The wall height varies from 15 meters high (left side) to 25 meters (right side). Big, easy to find holds on a moderate incline make this one of the more popular places for beginners.

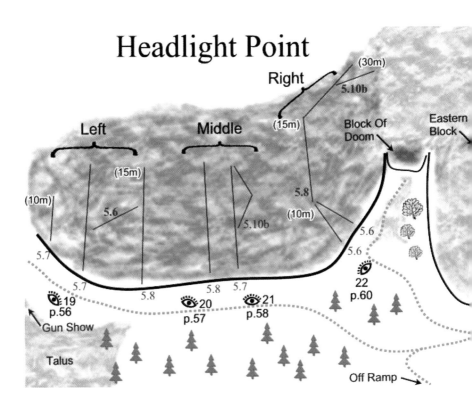

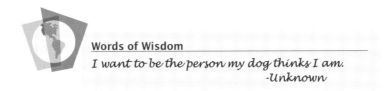

Words of Wisdom

I want to be the person my dog thinks I am.

-Unknown

Difficulty	Route	Bolts	Rating	Name
5.7	A	3	★★	Swerve
5.6	B	2	★★	In The Middle Again
5.7	C	4	★★	Midnight Scrambler
5.8	D	4	★★	Light-Headed Again

☐ Swerve _____ Date _____

☐ In The Middle Again _____ Date _____

☐ Midnight Scrambler _____ Date _____

☐ Light-Headed Again _____ Date _____

5.7
E

5.8
D

Eastern Block

👁 20 p.55

Difficulty	Route	Bolts	Rating	Name
5.8	E	6	★★★	Nocturnal Remission
5.7	F	5	★★★	Swarm

☐ Nocturnal Remission _____ Date _____

☐ Swarm _____ Date _____

👁 21 p.55

Difficulty	Route	Bolts	Rating	Name
5.7	F	5	★★	Swarm
5.10b	G	6	★★	Carnage Before Bedtime

☐ Swarm _____ Date _____

☐ Carnage Before Bedtime _____ Date _____

Right - Tina, warming up the focus,
on *"A Summer Known As Fall"* – 5.8 (p.205)

5.10b
K

5.8
J

5.6
I

5.6
H

Cave

Eastern Block

22 p.55

Headlight Point

Difficulty	Route	Bolts	Rating	Name
5.6	H	3	★★	Eating Rocks
5.6	I	3	★★	Eating Dust
5.8	J	10	★★★	Insomniac
5.10b	K	5 (Pro to 3")	★★	Bicycling To Bellingham ! See #7 p.106

☐ Eating Rocks_____

_____ Date _____

☐ Eating Dust_____

_____ Date _____

☐ Insomniac_____

_____ Date _____

☐ Bicycling To Bellingham _____

_____ Date _____

Words of Wisdom

It is not because things are difficult that we do not dare. It is because we do not dare that they are difficult.

- Lucius Annaeus Seneca

Eastern Block is the major rock wall between Squishy Bell and Headlight Point at Interstate Park. The entire wall is a unique series of interwoven blocks which make for some interesting, forget the fancy foot work and just crank, climbing.

The right section of the wall is nearly vertical but because of the abundance of monster jugs its difficulty is only around 5.7 – 5.9. The middle section is overhanging with a mini roof at the top but, again, because of those wonderfully fat holds, the routes are mostly in the 5.8 to 5.10 range.

The left side of the Eastern Block has a couple of unique climbs with an interesting feature affectionately referred to as the "Block of Doom". Step into the cave, look up, and you'll quickly understand the name. The cave does have the most unique sport route in the area. You have to climb out of the cave via a hole to reach the anchor!

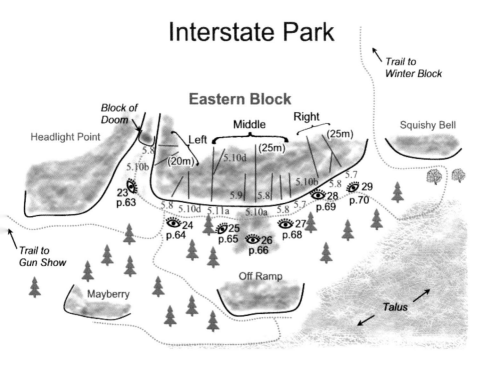

Eastern Block - Left

Block of Doom

5.8
A

5.10b
B

23 p.62

Difficulty	Route	Bolts	Rating	Name	
5.8	A	5	★★★	Tunnel Of Love	! See #5 p.106
5.10b	B	6	★★	Lip Service	

☐ Tunnel Of Love_____ Date _____

☐ Lip Service _____ Date _____

Difficulty	Route	Bolts	Rating	Name
5.8	D	6	★★	Impartial Eclipse
5.10c	E	6	★★	Space Face

☐ Impartial Eclipse _____ Date _____

☐ Space Face _____ Date _____

Cave

Headlight Point & Off Ramp

5.11a
F

5.10d
G

Step Up

👁 25 p.62

Difficulty	Route	Bolts	Rating	Name
5.11a	F	9	★ ★	Strategic Placement
5.10d	G	9	★ ★	Displacement ❗ See #6 p.106

☐ Strategic Placement _____ Date _____

☐ Displacement _____ Date _____

Deceased Tree

5.7
L

5.8
K

5.8
J

Step Down

5.10a
I

Rocky Area

5.9
H

Top of Off Ramp Wall

👁 26 p.62

Words of Wisdom

It is often easier to fight for one's principles than to live up to them. —Adlai Stevenson

Eastern Block - Middle

Far Side

Difficulty	Route	Bolts	Rating	Name
5.9	H	5	★	EB-1
5.10a	I	6	★★★	Ellie's Sweet Kiss
5.8	J	4	★	EB-2
5.8	K	4	★	EB-3
5.7	L	3	★	EB-4

☐ EB-1 _____

_____ Date _____

☐ Ellie's Sweet Kiss _____

_____

_____

_____ Date _____

☐ EB-2 _____

_____ Date _____

☐ EB-3 _____

_____ Date _____

☐ EB-4 _____

_____ Date _____

Words of Wisdom

Hope is a thing with feathers that perches in the soul.   *-Emily Dickinson*

5.7
L

5.8
M

Squishy Bell

👁 27 p.62

Difficulty	Route	Bolts	Rating	Name
5.7	L	3	★	EB-5
5.8	M	7	★★	EB-6

☐ EB-5 _____ Date _____

☐ EB-5 _____ Date _____

Eastern Block - Right

Far Side

5.10b
N

👁 28 p.62

Difficulty	Route	Bolts	Rating	Name
5.10b	N	8	★★★	Missing The Taco

☐ Missing The Taco _____ Date _____

5.8
O

Large Flake

5.7
P

👁 29 p.62

Difficulty	Route	Bolts	Rating	Name
5.8	O	8	★★★	Attack Of The Butter Knives
5.7	P	7	★★★★	Kiss Of The Crowbar

☐ Attach Of The Butter Knives_____ Date _____

☐ Kiss Of The Crowbar _____ Date _____

Marissa and Dan preparing for the wedding
on *"The Tunnel Of Love"* – 5.8 (p. 63)

Squishy Bell is the smallest of the three walls on the right side of Interstate Park. It has four petite routes from 5.5 – 5.9 which are all good "first time outdoor climbing" routes.

One of the pleasantly squishy things about the Bell is the routes can easily be top roped. This means that if you can't afford draws, or just don't want to be over burdened with the extra 4.5 pounds of rope weight, you can still enjoy some rock climbing. To reach the chains simply hike up the left side and around to the top.

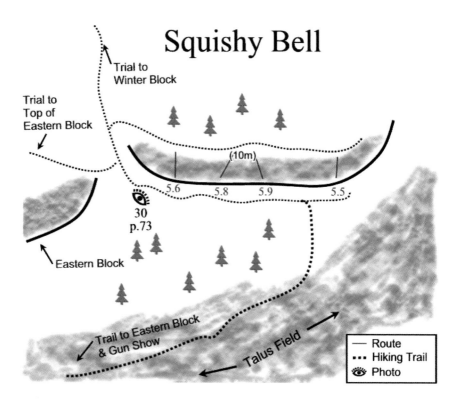

Squishy Bell

Far Side

👁 **30 p.72**

Difficulty	Route	Bolts	Rating	Name
5.6	A	2	★★	Catatonic
5.8	B	4	★★	Winter Rushing In
5.9	C	4	★★★	November Glaze
5.5	D	2	★★	Sumptuous Bits

☐ Catatonic _____

_____ Date _____

☐ Winter Rushing In _____

_____ Date _____

☐ November Glaze _____

_____ Date _____

☐ Sumptuous Bits _____

_____ Date _____

Off-Ramp is a short wall just below the middle of Interstate Park. If the main wall gets out of control, exit to Off-Ramp, kick back, and enjoy several puzzling routes.

One thing you'll notice is that Off-Ramp has seen some hard times i.e. bolt scars. I guess some people find putting others in danger entertaining. If you discover any route vandalism, send an email to info@northbendrock.com and it will be repaired as soon as possible.

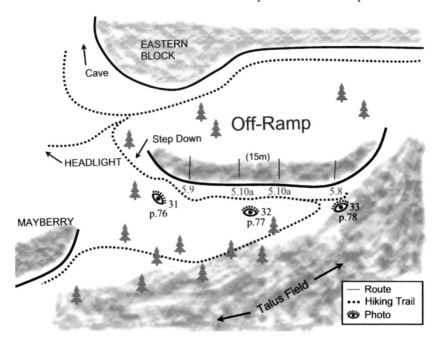

Never leave your wallet and credit cards in the car, unless you are so far in debt that it doesn't matter.   -Mr. GotRipped

To get to Off-Ramp, take the first off ramp (side trail) to the right just past Headlight Point after the trail goes up a short hill. Follow this trail 15 meters down to the bottom left side of the wall.

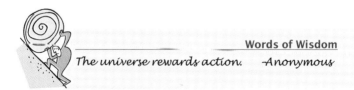

Words of Wisdom

The universe rewards action.   *—Anonymous*

5.9
A

👁 31 p.74

Difficulty	Route	Bolts	Rating	Name	
5.9	A	3	★★	Hit And Run	❗ See #8 p.106

☐ Hit And Run _____ Date _____

32 p.74

Difficulty	Route	Bolts	Rating	Name
5.10a	B	4	★★	Boys Drool
5.10a	C	5	★★★	Girls Rule!

☐ Girls Rule! _____

_____

_____ Date _____

☐ Boys Drool _____

_____

_____ Date _____

5.8
D

👁 33 p.74

Difficulty	Route	Bolts	Rating	Name
5.8	D	4	★★	Jersey Barrier

☐ Jersey Barrier _____

_____ Date _____

The Hand, making the crimp on
"Girls Rule" – 5.10a (p. 77)

Mayberry

Mayberry is a quite little wall below Interstate Park just to the left of Off-Ramp. Most climbers are pleasantly surprised to discover it because it's so close to the main trail but well hidden.

If it just happens that Off-Ramp is backed up then keep going to Mayberry.

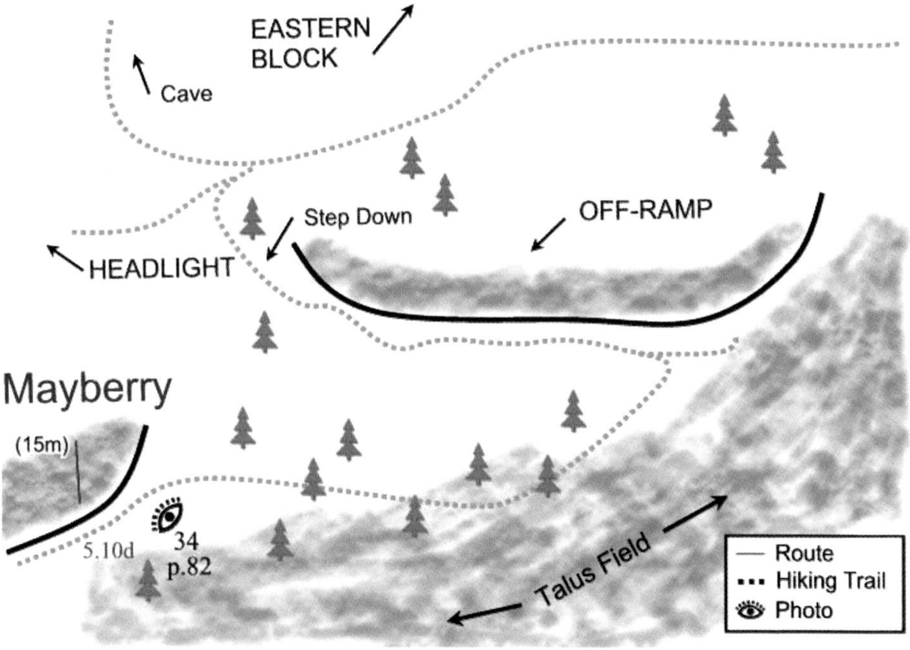

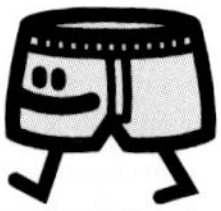

Tech Tip

Are your climbing shoes a good definition for "rude?" Putting dryer sheets in them can help. Putting the dryer sheets in your shorts for that third day without a shower, won't help.

Getting to Mayberry

Far Side

To get to Mayberry, take the side trail to Off-Ramp wall and scramble down 15 meters to the bottom section of the wall (map on p. 74). Follow the trail from the bottom of Off-Ramp wall for 30 meters to the talus field and around to the bottom right side of wall.

XX

5.10d
A

Off-Ramp

👁 34 p.80

Difficulty	Route	Bolts	Rating	Name
5.10d	A	5	★ ★	MB-1

☐ MB-1 _____

Right – Markus, enjoying some indoor climbing at
The Sammamish Club.   Photo by Mikaila Fulfs

Easy Street

Far Side

If you're just starting the Northwest climbing thing then Easy Street is a good place to visit. The surface of the rock is like course sandpaper and, at 45 degrees angle, beginning level climbers won't freak.

It's also a good place for beginners to learn how to climb a multi-pitch route. An instructor can climb the far right route, tie into the shared anchor, and assist a second climber without being on the route.

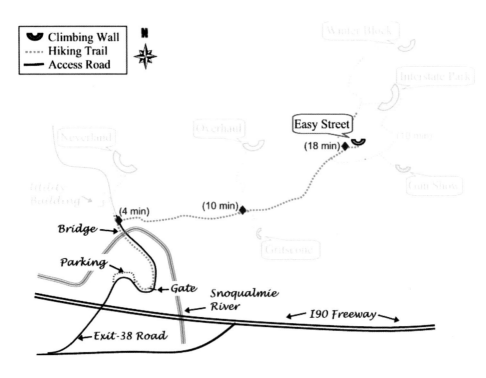

Words of Wisdom

Courage is not the absence of fear but rather the judgment that something else is more important than fear.   -Ambrose Redmoon

The routes start in the middle of a slab so you need to be careful crossing and belaying on the narrow ledge. There are belay anchor bolts so use them if you think your mother would tell you to.

EASY STREET

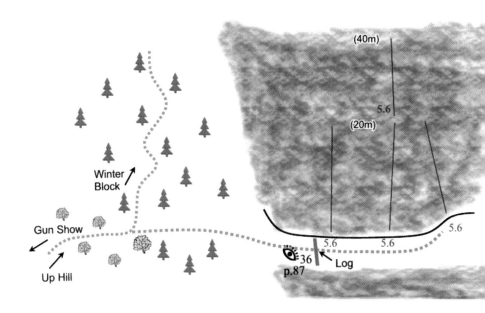

Did Ya Know?

Climbing shoe resolers can customize your new sole i.e. rand. For example, if you consistently wear out the inside section of your shoes then they can add additional rand for better durability.

Continue on the main trail, up a short hill, another 5 minutes past the Gun Show side trail.

Hike across the ridge 100 meters on the side trail to the left section of the wall. The routes begin just on the other side of a large log.

Easy Street

Difficulty	Route	Bolts	Rating	Name
5.6	A	6	★★★	ES-1
5.6	B	7	★★★	ES-2 (2 Pitches) ❗ See #12 p.107
5.6	C	13	★★	ES-3

☐ ES-1_____

_____ Date _____

☐ ES-2_____

_____ Date _____

☐ ES-3_____

_____ Date _____

If you're into flying kites and climbing, this could be your wall of nirvana. At 2373 feet elevation, Winter Block is the most distant and the highest crag in the Far Side area. Like Squishy Bell, it faces southeast on the ridge line for splendid views of McClellan's Butte and the modern concrete trail, referred to as Interstate 90, to the South.

Of all the walls at Far Side Winter Block gets the fewest visitors. Reason – there only four routes mostly in the range of 5.10 – 5.11 and it's a moderate 35 minute hike. So, if you're a climber who likes a little solitude, head on up and if you don't get the pump you need stop by Interstate Park on the way down.

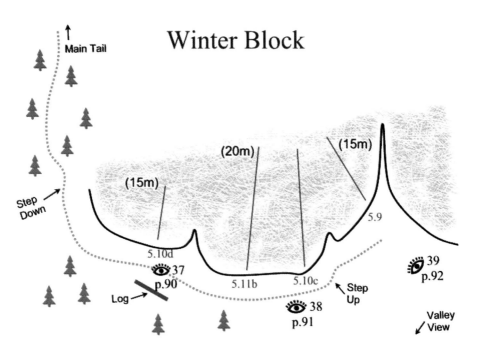

To get to Winter Block, follow the main trail up the ridge for 30 minutes (1.8 miles) and take the side trail to the right.

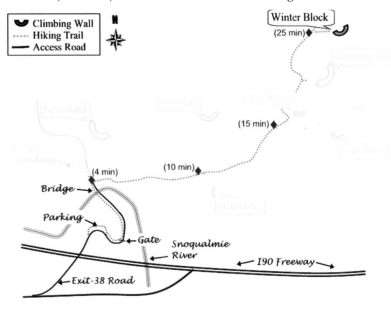

Follow the side trial for 100 meters and scramble down a short section along the right side of the crag to reach the base. *GPS Coordinate for trail turnoff: N 47.25.97 by W 121.37.21*

Main Trail

5.10d
A

👁 37 p.88

Difficulty	Route	Bolts	Rating	Name
5.10d	A	3	★ ★	Seismic Mardi Gras

☐ Seismic Mardi Gras _____ Date _____

38 p.88

Difficulty	Route	Bolts	Rating	Name
5.11b	B	5	★★	Of Gossamer Shrouds
5.10c	C	5	★★	Winter Walk Within

☐ Of Gossamer Shrouds _____ Date _____

☐ Winter Walk Within _____ Date _____

5.9
D

Main Trail

👁 39 p.88

Difficulty	Route	Bolts	Rating	Name
5.9	D	4	★★★	And The Sun Will Never Rise Again

☐ And The Sun Will Never Rise Again_____ Date _____

Michael and Gordy climbing in the rain on
"And The Sun Will Never Rise Again" – 5.9 (p. 92)

Neverland

Neverland is the newest addition to the Far Side climbing family. It's a large rocky ridge, visible to the North from the parking area, that's about 400 meters wide and 70 meters high. The climbing walls are, primarily a series of abrupt cliffs at the base of the ridge.

Neverland has 16 sport routes that range from 5.4 to 5.11a. The routes vary from inverted juggy face climbs to smooth slab routes. It also has several great multi-pitch routes and hanging belays for that extra adrenaline boost.

Make sure you bring your helmet. Don't just sit on it or leave it in your pack, put it on your head. The reason, other than the obvious one, is Neverland was created in 2005 and there will be loose rock until it has had a couple years of traffic and route development has slowed down.

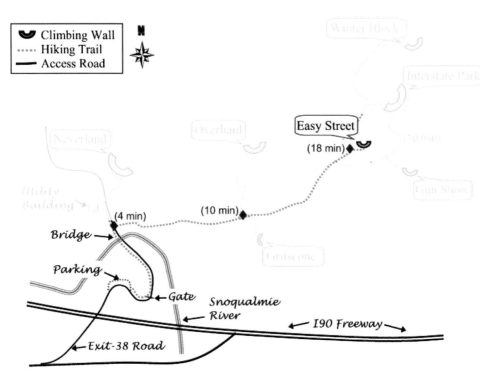

You might expect Neverland to get the same sun as the other Far Side routes but not true. Neverland is slightly rotated to the west so it gets its sun around 11:00am in the summer days, making it a great place to climb on hot mornings or in the afternoon on cool days.

Each of the four climbing areas of the Far Side is unique. For Gritscone it's convenient top roping. Gun Show has a nice slab route. Interstate Park has variety. Winter Block has... a long hike, and Neverland has several excellent multi-pitch routes, with complimentary hanging belays.

Neverland is the most recent area to be developed so there will most likely be several more routes added in the future. Check www.northbendrock.com for the latest route updates.

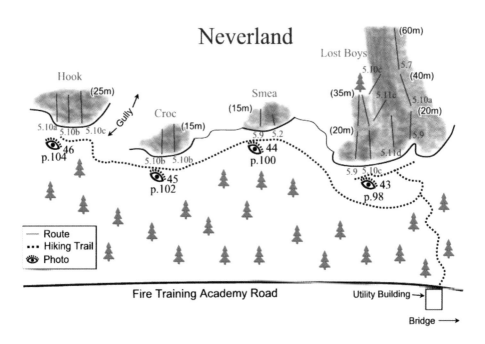

To get to Neverland, hike up the Fire Training Academy road from the lower parking area (5 minutes). The trail starts on the right side of the road directly across from a utility building next to a road marker.

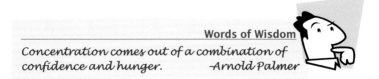

Words of Wisdom

Concentration comes out of a combination of confidence and hunger. —Arnold Palmer

Dave Perkins, making the clip, on the third pitch of
"The Plank" – 5.7 (p. 99)

Trail

Tree Stump

1st Pitch
5.9 - F

5.11d
F

2nd Pitch
5.10a - G

1st Pitch
5.10c - B

5.11c
C

1st Pitch
5.9 - A

3rd Pitch
5.7 - H

2nd Pitch
5.10c - B

5.10c
D

Old Tree

2nd Pitch
5.9 - A

43 p.95

Lost Boys

Far Side

Difficulty	Route	Bolts	Rating	Name	
5.9	A	12	★★★	I Wanna Go Home (2 pitches)	
5.10c	B	13	★★★	Lost My Marbles (2 pitches)	
5.11c	C	7	★★★	I Can Fly!	! See #14 p.107
5.10c	D	7	★★★	Sleep Or Awake?	
5.11d	E	7	★★★	Seize The Day	
5.9	F	7	★★★	The Plank (1st Pitch)	
5.10a	G	8	★★★	The Plank (2st Pitch)	! See #15 p.107
5.7	H	7	★★★★	The Plank (3rd Pitch)	! See #16 p.107

☐ I Wannna Go Home _____ Date _____

☐ Lost My Marbles _____ Date _____

☐ I Can Fly! _____ Date _____

☐ Sleep Or Awake? _____ Date _____

☐ Seize The Day _____ Date _____

☐ The Plank (1st Pitch) _____
_____ Date _____

☐ The Plank (2st Pitch) _____
_____ Date _____

☐ The Plank (3rd Pitch) _____
_____ Date _____

Lost Boys →

Croc ←

44 p. 95

Difficulty	Route	Bolts	Rating	Name
5.9	A	6	★★★	The Hamster
5.2	B	3	★★	Believe In Smea

☐ The Hamster _____ Date _____

☐ Believe in Smea _____ Date _____

Danielle, doing her first lead, on
"Believe in Smea" – 5.2 (p. 100)

Difficulty	Route	Bolts	Rating	Name
5.10b	A	5	★★	Bite Me
5.10b	B	5	★★★	Tick Tock

☐ Bite Me _____ Date _____

☐ Tick Tock _____ Date _____

Dave Argento, taking his time, on
"*Tick Tock*" – 5.10b (p. 102)

XX   XX   XX

5.10a
A

5.10b
B

5.10c
C

👁 46 p. 95

Hook

Difficulty	Route	Bolts	Rating	Name
5.10a	A	5	★★★	Hard To Port
5.10b	B	5	★★★	Pixie Dust Recommended
5.10c	C	5	★★★	Think Happy Thoughts

☐ Hard To Port _____

_____

_____ Date _____

☐ Pixie Dust Recommended _____

_____

_____ Date _____

☐ Think Happy Thoughts _____

_____

_____ Date _____

Words of Wisdom

When you cease to make a contribution, you begin to die.   -Eleanor Roosevelt

Most of the routes at the Far Side are safe e.g. clean rock, no trails above walls, recently bolted, etc. but some of the routes can be dangerous. Below is a list of additional safety considerations you need to be aware of if you climb on these routes.

#	Name	Warning
1	False Pretense 5.7 p. 26	Potential pendulum fall given route traverses arête. Rappel is free hanging.
2	Moreplay 5.11a p. 31	Another potential pendulum fall on roof traverse. Rope drag.
3	On The Outskirts 5.8 p. 32	Ridge traverse with potential swings if you fall. Need to climb twice to retrieve gear.
4	End Run 5.9 p. 35	Significant rope drag. Use long runners on initial hangers to help minimize.
5	Tunnel Of Love 5.8 p. 63	Cannot hear climber at chains. Lowers off via Lip Service route, to the right, so make sure it's clear.
6	Displacement 5.10d p. 65	Rope drag significant. Use long runners on top section.
7	Bicycling To Bellingham 5.10b p. 61	Rope drag from lower 5.6 route. Curves around and up ridge. Use longer runners or belay from top of 5.6 routes.
8	Hit and Run 5.9 p. 76	Tree's close to route. Don't forget about it on rappel.
9	Elation At The End Of... 5.8 p. 48	Difficult to impossible to hear climber. Bring radios or work out rope signals to communicate.
10	Web Slinger 5.10d p. 51	Getting to the route can be more dangerous than climbing it i.e. steep trail. Can't hear climber on second pitch.
11	Endless Bliss 5.10a p. 49	Traffic noise from freeway and wind make it hard to hear the climber on the first pitch and impossible on the second pitch. A bit run out on the second pitch, compared to 1st pitch. Most climbers rate it a 5.9, not a 5.10a.

#	Name	Warning
12	ES-2 5.6 p. 87	There is a narrow belay ledge. Clip into the hanger at waist level when belaying. Need to drag a rope or rap twice if you climb the second pitch.
13	GS-4 5.10b p. 47	Half way up the route there is an optional 5.10c branch to the chains of GS-3.
14	I Can Fly 5.11c p.99	Start via first pitch of "Lost My Marbles".
15	The Plank (2nd Pitch) 5.10b p.99	Easier to rappel to the top of "Seize The Day" route, instead of rappelling to the first pitch of "The Plank". Also, the belayer can not hear the climber so work out your signals or use radios.
16	The Plank (3rd Pitch) 5.7 p.99	You can swing off the edge, if you try, on the rappel. If so, simply lower to the chains on "Lost My Marbles" route.
17	GS-3 5.8 p.46	Rappel is to base of GS-4 route given route angles to the right. Need to climb it twice to retrieve draws.
18	GS-6 5.8 p. 47	Difficult to impossible to hear climber given freeway noise. Bring radios or work out rope signals to communicate.

Words of Wisdom

There is no rose without thorns.   *Antonio Pigafetta*

Best Far Side Routes

For those of you who wish you could climb more but can't take more time off work because you owe too much, here are the routes you've got to climb before your job kills you.

Diff.	Name		Wall	Stats	
5.6	ES-1	p.87	Easy Street	□ Lead □ Top Rope	□ Redpoint □ Flash
	ES-2	p. 87	Easy Street	□ Lead □ Top Rope	□ Redpoint □ Flash
5.7	Kiss Of The Crowbar	p. 70	Eastern Block	□ Lead □ Top Rope	□ Redpoint □ Flash
	The Plank (3rd Pitch)	p.99	Lost Boys	□ Lead □ Top Rope	□ Redpoint □ Flash
5.8	Nocturnal Remission	p.57	Eastern Block	□ Lead □ Top Rope	□ Redpoint □ Flash
	Attach Of The Butter Knives	p. 70	Eastern Block	□ Lead □ Top Rope	□ Redpoint □ Flash
5.9	The Plank (1st Pitch)	p.99	Neverland	□ Lead □ Top Rope	□ Redpoint □ Flash
	Elation At The End Eternity	p. 48	Gun Show	□ Lead □ Top Rope	□ Redpoint □ Flash
5.10a	Ellie's Sweet Kiss	p. 67	Eastern Block	□ Lead □ Top Rope	□ Redpoint □ Flash
	Endless Bliss	p.49	Gun Show	□ Lead □ Top Rope	□ Redpoint □ Flash
5.10b	Tick Tock	p.102	Croc	□ Lead □ Top Rope	□ Redpoint □ Flash
	Missing The Taco	p.69	Eastern Block	□ Lead □ Top Rope	□ Redpoint □ Flash
5.10c	Sleep or Awake?	p. 99	Lost Boys	□ Lead □ Top Rope	□ Redpoint □ Flash
	Mr. Fixit	p.23	Relief Camp	□ Lead □ Top Rope	□ Redpoint □ Flash
5.10d	I Can Fly!	p. 99	Lost Boys	□ Lead □ Top Rope	□ Redpoint □ Flash
	Jugular Vein	p. 25	Relief Camp	□ Lead □ Top Rope	□ Redpoint □ Flash
5.11a	Moreplay	p.30	Motherland	□ Lead □ Top Rope	□ Redpoint □ Flash
	Give Until It Hurts	p. 25	Relief Camp	□ Lead □ Top Rope	□ Redpoint □ Flash

1/2 – 1 Day, Beginning Level (5.6 – 5.8)

The Far Side has several great beginning level places to climb but to get the most stone for your shoes you should stay in the Interstate Park area.

Summary

Round Trip Time	5 ½ hours from Seattle
Hike	Moderate – 20 minutes, ¾ mile
Elevation Gain	503 feet
Best Season	Spring - Fall
Routes	Swerve, Swarm, Kiss of the Crowbar, ES-2
Notes	Start at Headlight Point and loop up and around to Easy Street for some guaranteed fun.

Details

Directions	Page	Time
Drive to Far Side parking area	16	35 min from Seattle
Hike to Headlight Point at Interstate Park	52	30 min
Warm up by climbing Swerve (5.7)	56	40 min
Continue up the trail 30 meters and do Swarm (5.7)	57	40 min
Continue up the trail another 5 minutes to the end of Eastern Block wall for Kiss Of The Crowbar (5.7)	70	45 min
Keep following the trail up and around past Squishy Bell wall to the Winter Block trail.	72	5 min
Head left and down to Easy Street side trail.	84	5 min
Climb the 1st and 2nd pitch of ES-2 (5.6)	87	60 min
Hike back to parking area	15	15 min
Call your friends and tell them you want to quit your job and travel around the world rock climbing.	---	---

1/2 – 1 Day, Intermediate Level (5.9 – 5.10c)

Each area has some excellent intermediate climbs but, to get the most adrenaline for the short time, head to Neverland Wall.

Summary

Round Trip Time	5 hours from Seattle
Hike	Easy – 8 minutes, ¼ mile
Elevation Gain	200 feet
Best Season	Spring - Fall
Routes	I Wanna Go Home, The Plank
Notes	Second rappel is to top of 5.10c route. If you lower over the edge from the top, rappel from the Plank route chains.

Details

Directions	Page	Time
Drive to Far Side parking area	16	35 min from Seattle
Hike to the base of Lost Boys wall at Neverland	94	7 min
Climb to the first set of chains on the left route "I Wanna Go Home" (5.9)	99	30 min
Continue on to the second pitch on "I Wanna Go Home" (5.9)	99	30 min
Next, climb the first pitch of the multi-pitch route "The Plank" (5.9).	99	40 min
Continue to the second pitch up and around the edge. (5.10b).	99	40 min
Climb the third and final pitch of The Plank to the top. (5.7)	99	40 min
Rappel to the second pitch anchor	99	20 minutes
Rappel to the top of 11d route "Seize The Day" if it's available or step over to first pitch anchor and lower to start.	99	20 minutes
Hike back to parking area	16	5 min

1/2 – 1 Day, Advanced Level (5.10d – 5.12c)

There is really only one wall at Far Side for advanced climbers looking to shred the fingers and loosen the connective tissue: Overhaul.

Summary

Round Trip Time	6.5 hours (round trip from Seattle)
Hike	Moderate – 20 minutes, ¾ mile
Elevation Gain	800 feet
Best Season	Summer
Routes	Rhino Relief, Give Until It Hurts, Jugular Vein, Mr. Fixit, Chain Gang, Hovering Mother, Offspring
Notes	All single pitch routes, mostly overhanging jugs

Details

Directions	Page	Time
Drive to Far Side parking area	16	35 min from Seattle
Hike to Overhaul Wall	19	35 min
Warm up on "Rhino Relief" (5.10a)	25	40 min
Go straight for the burn just to the right Rhino Relief on "Give Until It Hurts" (5.11a)	25	40 min
Step right and pump'em up again on "Jugular Vein" (5.10d)	25	40 min
Bounce back left 20 paces for Mr. Fixit and Chain Gang	23	80 min
Crawl up the trail a dozen paces to the middle, Motherland section of the wall	18	5 min
Give it all up for "Hovering Mother" (5.12b) and end it with a final finally on "Offspring" (5.12b)	31	80 min
Stagger back to the parking area, stopping briefly at the river to cool the forearms	15	15 min

Far Side Route Listing

Diff.	Name		Wall	Diff.	Name		Wall
5.2	☐ ★ ★ Believe In Smea	p. 100	Smea	5.8	☐ ★ ★ Winter Rushing In	p. 73	Squishy Bell
5.5	☐ ★ ★ So Easy I Forgot to...	p. 41	Gritscone		☐ ★ ★ Chain Gain	p. 23	Relief Camp
	☐ ★ ★ Sumptuous Bits	p. 73	Squishy Bell		☐ ★ ★ Cornery Bypass	p. 29	Motherland
5.6	☐ ★ ★ ★ ES-1	p. 87	Easy Street		☐ ★ ★ Corner's Inquest	p. 29	Motherland
	☐ ★ ★ ★ ES-2	p. 87	Easy Street		☐ ★ ★ On The Outskirts	p. 32	Motherland
	☐ ★ ★ ES-3	p. 87	Easy Street		☐ ★ ★ GS-3	p. 46	Gun Show
	☐ ★ ★ Eating Dust	p. 61	Interstate Park		☐ ★ ★ GS-6	p. 47	Gun Show
	☐ ★ ★ Eating Rocks	p. 61	Headlight Point		☐ ★ ★ Jersy Barrier	p. 78	Off-Ramp
	☐ ★ ★ In The Middle Again	p. 56	Headlight Point		☐ ★ EB-2	p. 67	Eastern Block
	☐ ★ ★ Lucky Arms	p. 39	Gritscone		☐ ★ EB-3	p. 67	Eastern Block
	☐ ★ ★ Catatonic	p. 73	Squishy Bell		☐ ★ EB-6	p. 68	Eastern Block
5.7	☐ ★ ★ ★ ★ Kiss Of The...	p. 70	Eastern Block		☐ ★ GS-1	p. 45	Gun Show
	☐ ★ ★ ★ ★ The Plank (3rd Pitch)	p.99	Lost Boys		☐ ★ GS-2	p. 45	Gun Show
	☐ ★ ★ Swerve	p.56	Headlight Point	5.9	☐ ★ ★ ★ I Wanna Go Home	p. 99	Lost Boys
	☐ ★ ★ Swarm	p. 58	Headlight Point		☐ ★ ★ ★ The Plank(1st Pitch)	p. 99	Lost Boys
	☐ ★ ★ Midnight Scrambler	p. 56	Headlight Point		☐ ★ ★ ★ End Run	p. 35	Slabbage Patch
	☐ ★ ★ Pete's Possum...	p. 41	Gritscone		☐ ★ ★ ★ Siamese Dream	p. 35	Slabbage Patch
	☐ ★ ★ Party Girl	p.35	Slabbage Patch		☐ ★ ★ ★ 99 Grit	p. 41	Gritscone
	☐ ★ ★ Needle Magnet	p. 38	Gritscone		☐ ★ ★ ★ And The Sun Will...	p. 92	Winter Block
	☐ ★ ★ So Funny I Forgot. To...	p. 41	Gritscone		☐ ★ ★ ★ November Glaze	p. 73	Squishy Bell
	☐ ★ ★ False Pretense	p. 26	Motherland		☐ ★ ★ ★ Elation At The...	p. 48	Gun Show
	☐ ★ ★ Snaffle Baffler	p. 39	Gritscone		☐ ★ ★ ★ The Hamster	p. 100	Smean
	☐ ★ EB-4	p. 67	Eastern Block		☐ ★ ★ Hit and Run	p. 76	Off-Ramp
	☐ ★ EB-5	p. 68	Eastern Block		☐ ★ ★ GS-7	p. 49	Gun Show
5.8	☐ ★ ★ ★ Attack Of The...	p. 70	Eastern Block		☐ ★ ★ Magnetic Anomaly	p. 38	Gritscone
	☐ ★ ★ ★ Insomniac	p.61	Headlight Point		☐ ★ Nature Boy	p. 35	Slabbage Patch
	☐ ★ ★ ★ Nocturnal Remission	p. 57	Headlight Point		☐ ★ EB-1	p. 67	Eastern Block
	☐ ★ ★ ★ Tunnel Of Love	p. 63	Eastern Block				
	☐ ★ ★ Impartial Eclipse	p. 64	Eastern Block				
	☐ ★ ★ Light-Headed Again	p. 56	Headlight Point				

Far Side Route Listing

Diff.	Name		Wall	Diff.	Name		Wall
5.10a	☐ ★ ★ ★ Endless Bliss	p. 49	Gun Show	5.10d	☐ ★ ★ ★ Jugular Vein	p. 25	Relief Camp
	☐ ★ ★ ★ The Plank (2nd Pitch)	p.99	Lost Boys		☐ ★ ★ ★ Mr. Fixlt	p 23	Relief Camp
	☐ ★ ★ ★ Ellie's Sweet Kiss	p. 67	Eastern Block		☐ ★ ★ Web Slinger (2nd)	p. 51	Gun Show
	☐ ★ ★ ★ Girls Rule!	p. 77	Off-Ramp		☐ ★ ★ Displacement	p. 65	Eastern Block
	☐ ★ ★ ★ Chica Rapida	p. 40	Gritscone		☐ ★ ★ MB-1	p. 82	Mayberry
	☐ ★ ★ ★ Rhino Relief	p. 25	Relief Camp		☐ ★ ★ Seismic Mardi...	p. 90	Winter Block
	☐ ★ ★ ★ Web Slinger (1st)	p. 51	Gun Show		☐ ★ ★ Stretcher Case	p. 32	Motherland
	☐ ★ ★ ★ Hard To Port	p. 105	Hook		☐ ★ Super Squish	p. 49	Gun Show
	☐ ★ ★ Boys Drool!	p. 77	Off-Ramp	5.11a	☐ ★ ★ ★ Moreplay	p. 31	Motherland
	☐ ★ ★ Shelf Serve	p. 23	Relief Camp		☐ ★ ★ ★ Give Until It Hurts	p. 25	Relief Camp
	☐ ★ ★ Toying With...	p. 29	Motherland		☐ ★ ★ Strategic Placement	p. 65	Eastern Block
5.10b	☐ ★ ★ ★ Missing The Taco	p. 69	Eastern Block		☐ ★ ★ A Girl's Best Friend	p. 40	Gritscone
	☐ ★ ★ ★ Tick Tock	p.102	Croc		☐ ★ ★ Foreplay	p. 29	Motherland
	☐ ★ ★ ★ Sheltered...	p. 29	Motherland	5.11b	☐ ★ ★ ★ Chain Gang	p. 23	Relief Camp
	☐ ★ ★ ★ Pixie Dust...	p.105	Hook		☐ ★ ★ Complete Overhaul	p. 23	Relief Camp
	☐ ★ ★ Bite Me	p.102	Croc		☐ ★ ★ Of Gossamer Shrouds	p. 91	Winter Block
	☐ ★ ★ Bicycling To...	p. 61	Headlight Point	5.11c	☐ ★ ★ ★ I Can Fly!	p. 99	Lost Boys
	☐ ★ ★ Carnage Before...	p. 58	Headlight Point		☐ ★ GS-10	p.50	Gun Show
	☐ ★ ★ Lip Service	p. 63	Eastern Block	5.11d	☐ ★ ★ ★ Sieze The Day	p. 99	Relief Camp
	☐ ★ ★ GS-4	p. 47	Gun Show		☐ ★ Rough Cut	p. 39	Gritscone
	☐ ★ Controlled Bleeding	p.25	Relief Camp		☐ ★ GS-8	p. 49	Gun Show
5.10c	☐ ★ ★ ★ Sleep or Awake?	p.99	Lost Boys	5.12a	☐ ★ ★ ★ Offspring	p. 31	Motherland
	☐ ★ ★ ★ Lost My Marbles	p.99	Lost Boys	5.12b	☐ ★ ★ ★ Hovering Mother	p. 31	Motherland
	☐ ★ ★ ★ Think Happy...	p. 105	Hook		☐ ★ Ghost	p. 21	Relief Camp
	☐ ★ ★ Winter Walk Within	p.91	Winter Block		☐ ★ Flubber	p. 26	Relief Camp
	☐ ★ ★ Space Face	p. 64	Eastern Block	5.12c	☐ ★ Green Lantern	p. 21	Relief Camp
	☐ ★ ★ GS-9	p. 50	Gun Show				
	☐ ★ ★ GS-5	p. 47	Gun Show				
	☐ ★ ★ Booty Squirrel	p. 40	Gritscone				

Deception Crags

Of the three climbing areas at Exit 38 (Far Side, Deception Crags, and Mt. Washington) Deception Crags is the most popular. The key reason: it was developed for the newer breed of quick gratification, don't have much time, rock climber. Simple to find, straightforward route access, single pitch, and many good beginner routes ensure it will remain popular.

There are six places to climb at Deception: Substation; Write-Off, Nevermind, Deception Wall, We Did Rock, and Hall Creek Rock. Substation, Write-Off, and We Did Rock offer the most beginner routes (5.5 - 5.9). Deception Wall is mostly intermediate routes (5.10 - 5.11). Nevermind is advanced climbing (5.11 - 5.12).

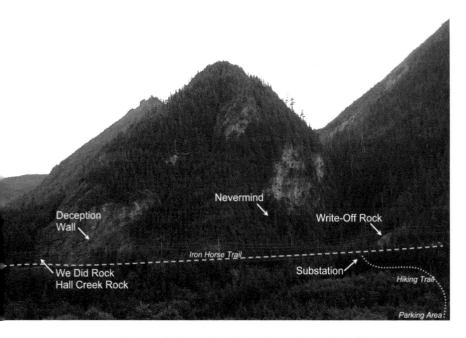

Picture of Deception Area from Interstate-90

Over half of the routes at Deception start from narrow bridges or ledges that were built alongside the rock walls for the train tracks when it wasn't feasible to create a tunnel. These narrow trails can quickly get congested with climbers, hikers, and bikers, especially on the weekends, so please keep your belay area tidy and off to the side of the trail.

This photo was taken from the East bound lane of Interstate 90 freeway. The parking area is in the lower right side of the picture, just out of view. The distance from Write-Off Rock on the right side of the picture to We Did Rock on the left side is about 1/8 mile, a 5 minute hike.

Deception Crags is part of not one, but two State Parks: Ollalie State Park and Iron Horse State Park. The Ollalie State Park encompasses a portion of the South Fork of the Snoqualmie River. The park provides trails along the river. The parking for these trails is shared with the parking for the Deception Climbing area. Iron Horse State park is the old Milwaukee Railroad bed. (For more information about either of the parks see http://www.parks.wa.gov)

There are several rules and guidelines which govern the climbing areas in these State Parks. The most important being – no overnight camping or bivouacs, groups of 10 or more must have a permit, and fee based climbing classes must have a commercial permit.

Words of Wisdom

A ship in a harbor is safe, but that's not what ships are built for.   -*Unknown*

Area Summary

To summarize the summary, there are a lot of diverse single pitch sport routes in a small area just waiting to fulfill your every climbing need.

Wall Name	Height (Meters)	# of Routes	Hiking Time (Minutes)	Elev. Gain (Feet)
Substation	15	18	5	150
Kiosk Rock	5	1	8	200
Write-Off Rock	10	5	7	200
Nevermind	20	20	10	225
Deception Wall	75	13	10	200
We Did Rock	15	9	13	200
Hall Creek Rock	10	4	13	200

Elevation Profile

This elevation profile shows you why this area is very popular – it's only a couple hundred feet of elevation gain up a gradual creek basin making it the quickest and easiest to access.

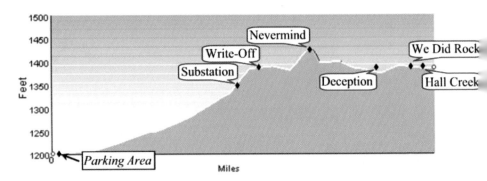

Wall and Route Difficulty

The primary purpose of the following chart is to look cool. The secondary purpose is to show you which walls have the most routes you can climb. For example, if you're just getting started in the rock climbing world then Write-Off Rock has the easiest routes. On the other hand, if you're a 5.10+ climber then Nevermind Wall would be a great place to visit.

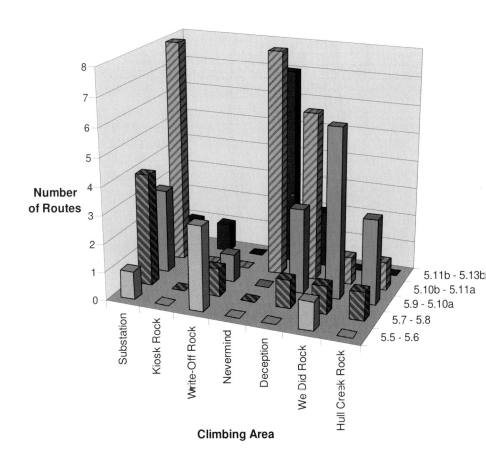

You'll find the Deception Crags parking area (in the middle of the map below) on the left side of the paved road .5 miles after taking eastbound Exit 38 from Interstate 90 (state map on p. 9).

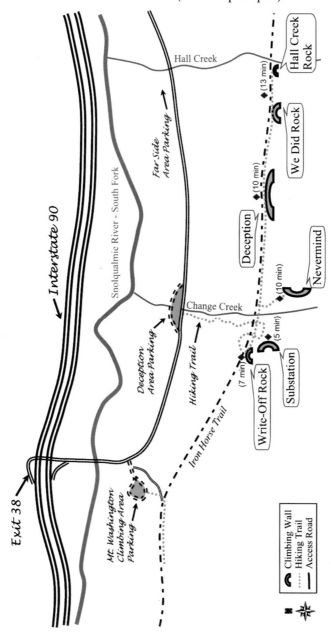

Parking at Deception

The parking area for Deception Crags is actually the west bound lane of the old I-90 freeway. Needless to say, you shouldn't have a problem finding a spot to park, unless your climbing vehicle is a double trailer semi-truck.

Trail Head
Far Side (1 mile)
I-90 (.5 mile)
Parking Area

√ It Out

The Iron Horse trail, which is the starting point for most of the climbs at Deception, is part of a 100+ mile trail that extends from Cedar Falls to the Columbia River. The Change Creek trestle, which you hike under, is one of the few old railroad trestles still in existence.

Substation is the first crag you reach from the parking area. It has several great climbs for beginners as well as a number of choice intermediate routes. It also has the unique feature of a massive steel train trestle attached to its upper end.

Substation is a great place to loiter during the warm summer months given it stays cool because it's lower on the ridge and shaded by trees. During the spring and fall months the area between the left and right sections will be wet. In the winter you won't find any dry routes.

Substation

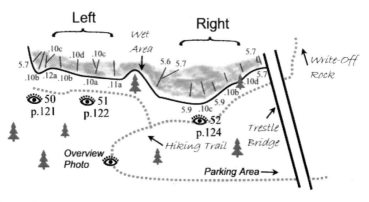

Deception

50 p.120

Difficulty	Route	Bolts	Rating	Name
5.7	A	6	★★	Turf Safari
5.10b	B	5	★	Bwana Be Your Man
5.12a	C	6	★	Stick Boy
5.10c	D	7	★★	Slippery When Wet

☐ Turf Safari _____ Date _____

☐ Bwana Be Your Man_____ Date _____

☐ Stick Boy _____ Date _____

☐ Slippery When Wet_____ Date _____

5.11a
I

5.10c
H

5.10a
G

5.10d
F

5.10d
E

5.10c
D

51 p.120

Substation - Left

Difficulty	Route	Bolts	Rating	Name
5.10c	D	7	★★	Slippery When Wet
5.10d	E	6	★★	You're Only Nice To Me When You're Wet
5.10d	F	7	★★	You're Only Nice To Me When I Tie You Up
5.10a	G	7	★★★	Lovey-Dovey
5.10c	H	6	★★	Namby-Pamby
5.11a	I	4	★★★	Hangover Helper

☐ Slippery When Wet _____

_____ Date _____

☐ You're Only Nice To Me When You're Wet _____

_____ Date _____

☐ You're Only Nice To Me When I Tie You Up _____

_____ Date _____

☐ Lovey-Dovey _____

_____ Date _____

☐ Namby-Pamby _____

_____ Date _____

☐ Hangover Helper _____

_____ Date _____

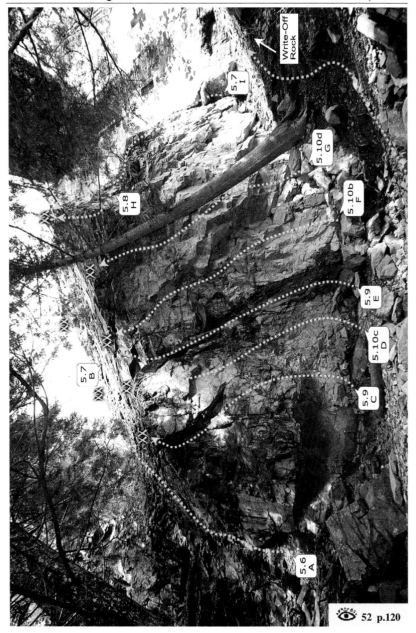

Write-Off Rock

5.7 I

5.10d G

5.10b F

5.8 H

5.9 E

5.10c D

5.7 B

5.9 C

5.6 A

👁 52 p.120

Difficulty	Route	Bolts	Rating	Name
5.6	A	6	★★★	Homo Erectus
5.7	B	6	★★★	Rug Monkey
5.9	C	2	★★	Primordial Blues
5.10c	D	3	★★	Chain Smoken
5.9	E	4	★★★	Hurly-Burly
5.10b	F	4	★★	Subliminal
5.10d	G	4	★★	Subversive
5.8 ↻	H	4	★★★	Glom Don
5.7 ↻	I	4	★★★	Glob Job

☐ Homo Erectus _____ Date _____

☐ Rug Monkey _____ Date _____

☐ Primordial Blues _____ Date _____

☐ Chain Smoken _____ Date _____

☐ Hurly-Burly _____ Date _____

☐ Subliminal _____ Date _____

☐ Subversive _____ Date _____

☐ Glom Don _____ Date _____

☐ Glob Job _____ Date _____

Write-Off Rock

Write-Off Rock is a great beginner's area. It's a short distance from the parking lot, easy to find, has good novice routes, pleasant views of the valley, and has a comfortable area for family and friends to watch. Needless to say, on warm summer weekends it gets a lot of traffic. To set a top rope on the routes, follow the trail up and around the lower left side of Substation to the top of Write-Off Rock.

Take care not to leave your backpack, rope, power bars, or the like on the Iron Horse Trail in front of the Rock. Bikers have a tendency to get irritated when they lose control of their bikes at high speeds after hitting trail obstacles they were not expecting.

Write-Off Rock

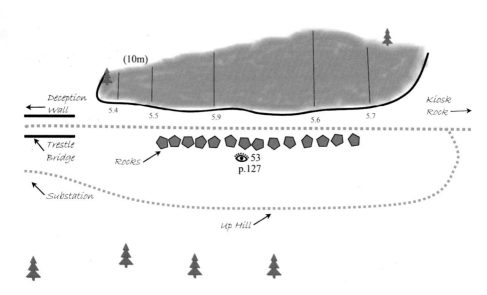

Trestle

5.4 A

5.5 B

5.9 C

5.6 D

5.7 E

← Iron Horse Trail →

👁 53 p.126

To Substation →

Difficulty	Route	Bolts	Rating	Name
5.4 ↻	A	3	★★	Bu The Rabbit
5.5 ↻	B	4	★★	Flammable Pajamas
5.9 ↻	C	5	★★	Knife In The Toaster
5.6	D	4	★★	Mom There's Pink In My Burger
5.7	E	5	★★	Bottoms Up

☐ Bu The Rabbit _____ _____ Date _____

☐ Flammable Pajamas_____ Date _____

☐ Knife In The Toaster_____ Date _____

☐ Mom There's Pink In My Burger _____ Date _____

☐ Bottoms Up _____ Date _____

Taylor, age 5, pulling the roof with dad (Dave) on
"Flammable Pajamas" – 5.5 (p. 127)

Kiosk Rock

Deception

Kiosk Rock is a small and lonely chunk of stone to the right of Write-Off Rock just past the Bulletin Board. It has one route. It has one move. It's had one climber.

XX

5.11b
A

Write-Off Rock

👁 54 p.126

Difficulty	Route	Bolts	Rating	Name
5.11b	A	2	★	Easy Money

☐ Easy Money _____ Date _____

Deception - 129

Nevermind

If you're an advanced climber (mostly 5.11 – 5.12) you'll appreciate Nevermind. It has fourteen clean, lean, and mean routes. The routes have great consistency, positive edges, and it's rarely crowded. The wall is slightly overhung and will stay mostly dry and climbable year round.

One of the things I enjoy about this wall is a spectacular old growth tree that starts below the wall and towers above it. It's truly an impressive sight and it's humbling to consider that the valley was once filled with old growth trees.

Nevermind Wall

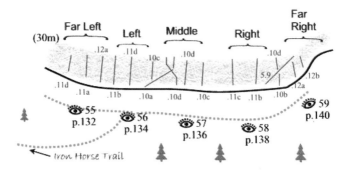

To get to Nevermind, turn left when you reach the Iron Horse trail from the parking lot. Continue past Write-Off Rock and over the trestle bridge. The side trail starts on your right just after crossing the trestle. The first part of the side trail is up a short rocky scramble with a small hand rope in the middle. It then meanders along the hillside for 300 yards before depositing you at the far left section of the wall.

Nevermind
Side Trail

Write-Off
Rock →

← Deception
Wall

👁 55 p.130

Difficulty	Route	Bolts	Rating	Name
5.11d	A	4	★★★	Rude Road
5.11a	B	5	★★★	Steep Street
5.12a	C	5	★★	Under Arrest
5.11b	D	9	★★★	Negatherion

☐ Rude Road_____ Date _____

☐ Steep Street_____ Date _____

☐ Under Arrest_____ Date _____

☐ Negatherion _____ Date _____

Deb belaying Jerome while he takes a moment to pray on
"Neverigine" – 5.10a (p.135)

5.11c
H

5.10c
G

5.10d
J

5.11d
E

5.10a
F

5.11b
D

56 p.130

Nevermind - Left

Difficulty	Route	Bolts	Rating	Name
5.11b	D	9	★★★	Negatherion
5.11d	E	7	★★	Corporeal Completion
5.10a	F	7	★★★	Neverigine
5.10c	G	4	★★	Powerless
5.11c	H	10	★★	Hangerville
5.10d	J	8	★★★	Easily Amused

☐ Negatherion _____

_____ Date _____

☐ Corporeal Completion _____

_____ Date _____

☐ Neverigine _____

_____ Date _____

☐ Powerless _____

_____ Date _____

☐ Hangerville _____

_____ Date _____

☐ Easily Amused _____

_____ Date _____

√ It Out

Recognize the huge trees around Nevermind wall? They're old growth Douglas Fir. The largest tree, behind the center of the wall, is around 150 years old. It was a seedling about the time Abraham Lincon was elected President.

Nevermind - Middle

👁 57 p.130

Difficulty	Route	Bolts	Rating	Name
5.10a	F	7	★★★	Neverigine
5.10d	J	8	★★★	Easily Amused
5.10c	K	7	★★★	Love Bucket
5.11a	M	10	★★★	Architect Rally

☐ Neverigine _____ Date _____

☐ Easily Amused _____ Date _____

☐ Love Bucket _____ Date _____

☐ Architect Rally _____ Date _____

Dave, spotting Melissa, at the first clip on
"Powerless" – 5.10c (p.135)

5.10d
P

5.10b
Q

5.9
O

5.11a
M

5.11c
N

5.10c
K

58 p.130

Difficulty	Route	Bolts	Rating	Name
5.10c	K	7	★★★	Love Bucket
5.11a	M	10	★★★	Architect Rally
5.11c	N	11	★★	Canine Patrol
5.9	O	7	★★	Strip Clip
5.10d	P	9	★★★	Big Mama
5.10b	Q	8	★	Strip Clip Direct

☐ Love Bucket _____

_____ Date _____

☐ Architect Rally _____

_____ Date _____

☐ Canine Patrol _____

_____ Date _____

☐ Strip Clip_____

_____ Date _____

☐ Big Mama_____

_____ Date _____

☐ Strip Clip Direct _____

_____ Date _____

59 p.130

Difficulty	Route	Bolts	Rating	Name
5.9	O	7	★ ★	Strip Clip
5.12a	R	9	★ ★	Culture Shock
5.12b	S	4	★ ★	The Goblet

☐ Strip Clip _____ Date _____

☐ Culture Shock _____ Date _____

☐ The Goblet _____ Date _____

Deception Wall

Deception

Deception Wall is the most dominate wall in the Deception Crags area, hence its name. It's about 200 meters wide and 100 meters high but only has a dozen or so routes given the rock type and precarious access. All that size isn't wasted though for it does have one multi-pitch route. In fact, it's the only multi-pitch route in the Deception area.

Most of the routes start directly from a long concrete bridge or shoulder on the Iron Horse Trail. This is convenient, but it doesn't leave much room for bikers and hikers to pass by on the trail so keep your belay station extra tidy.

Deception Wall

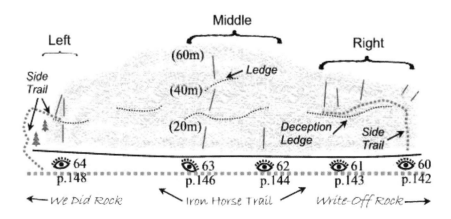

Left   Middle   Right

Side Trail

(60m)

Ledge

(40m)

(20m)

Deception Ledge

Side Trail

👁 64
p.148

👁 63
p.146

👁 62
p.144

👁 61
p.143

👁 60
p.142

← We Did Rock   Iron Horse Trail   Write-Off Rock →

Difficulty	Route	Bolts	Rating	Name
5.13b	K	4	★	Deliverance
5.13d	L	5	★	(Open Project)

☐ Deliverance _____ Date _____

☐ (Open Project) _____ Date _____

👁 61 p.141

Difficulty	Route	Bolts	Rating	Name	
5.12a	F	6	★★	The End	
5.11a	G	9	★★★	The Overture	❗See #1 p. 159
5.10c	H	5	★★★	The Underture	❗See #1 p. 159
5.10a	I	9	★★★	Won't Get Fooled Again	

☐ The End _____ Date _____

☐ The Overture _____ Date _____

☐ The Underture _____ Date _____

☐ Won't Get Fooled Again _____ Date _____

XX

5.9
G

👁 62 p.141

Iron Horse Trail →

Difficulty	Route	Bolts	Rating	Name
5.9	G	5	★★	Underground Economy! See #2 p. 159

☐ Underground Economy _____ Date _____

Local climbers getting it done on
"*Rat Face*" - 5.10c (left) and "*Underground Economy*" – 5.9 (right)

60 meters → XX

5.12a
F

40 meters → XX

25 meters → XX

5.10c
E

XX

Write-Off Rock

5.7
A

We Did Rock

👁 63 p.141

Difficulty	Route	Bolts	Rating	Name	
5.7	D	4	★★	Jiffy Pop	
5.10c	E	12	★★	Rat Face	❗ See #3 p. 159
5.12a	F	6	★★	The End	❗ See #4 p. 159

☐ Jiffy Pop _____ Date _____

☐ Rat Face _____ Date _____

☐ The End _____ Date _____

AJ Ritter watching the pretty girls go by on
"*Jiffy Pop*" – 5.7 (p.146)

5.11a
B
5.10a
C
Trail
5.10c
A
Side Trail to
Routes B & C
64 p.141

Difficulty	Route	Bolts	Rating	Name
5.10c	A	5	★	Side Dish
5.11a	B	6	★★★	Late for Dinner
5.10a	C	5	★★★★	Just Desert

☐ Side Dish ______________________ Date __________

☐ Late for Dinner ______________________ Date __________

☐ Just Desert ______________________ Date __________

We Did Rock

We Did Rock is the next series of rock faces just past Deception Wall to the East. It consists of a left and a right section. The right section begins just after crossing the concrete walk way from Deception Wall. The left section is 60 meters further down the Iron Horse trail.

We Did Rock is a fine piece of slab. The wall gathers a lot of beginning climbers because it's covered with excellent 5.9ish routes.

We Did Rock

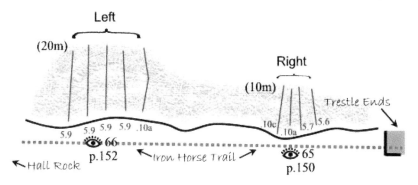

65 p.149

Difficulty	Route	Bolts	Rating	Name
5.10c	A	4	★	The Joke
5.10a	B	4	★	My X Wife (short and easy)
5.7	C	3	★	Your Sister
5.6	D	3	★★	Easy Street

☐ The Joke _____ Date _____

☐ My X Wife (short and easy) _____ Date _____

☐ Your Sister _____ Date _____

☐ Easy Street _____ Date _____

Jamie and Angela watching Wayne look for something on
"*Absolutely Nothing*" We Did Rock – 5.9 (p. 153)

5.10+
F

5.9
E

5.9
D

5.9
C

5.9
B

5.9
A

66 p.149

We Did Rock - Left

Deception

Difficulty	Route	Bolts	Rating	Name
5.9	A	6	★★	Black Caboose
5.9	B	6	★★	Sobriety
5.9	C	6	★★★★	Absolutely Nothing
5.9	D	6	★★★	Some Drugs
5.9	E	6	★★★	Blockhead
5.10+	F	-	-	(Open Project)

☐ Black Caboose _____

_____ Date _____

☐ Sobriety _____

_____ Date _____

☐ Absolutely Nothing _____

_____ Date _____

☐ Some Drugs _____

_____ Date _____

☐ Blockhead _____

_____ Date _____

☐ (Open Project) _____

_____ Date _____

Words of Wisdom

Be the change you wish to see in the world.   *-Gandhi*

Hall Creek Rock

Deception

Hall Creek Rock is a creatively named rock, 50 meters past We Did Rock. The routes are a recent addition to the area and the last of the Deception Crags climbs on the eastern side of the area. If We Did Rock is in demand, mosey down the trail and check out it.

The few routes on this rock aren't anything you'll be bragging to your friends about, but the rock is known for a couple of interesting reasons. It's the only known location in the entire Exit 38 climbing area to be credited with a reported climbing accident. The accident was on Erectile Dysfunction. The overly excited climber clipped the first two bolts, tried to clip the third, slipped, and grounded. Ouch. The second reason it's known is that it has the shortest sport route in the North Bend area, aptly named "Sport Sickness". It's about 5 meters high with two generous bolts.

Hall Creek Rock

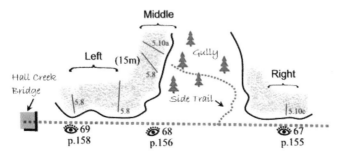

Deception - 154

Hall Creek Rock - Right

Deception

5.10c
E

Hall Creek Rock
(Middle)

67 p. 154

We Did Rock

Difficulty	Route	Bolts	Rating	Name
5.10c	D	2	★	Sport Sickness

☐ Sport Sickness _____ Date _____

Deception - 155

68 p.154

Difficulty	Route	Bolts	Rating	Name
5.9	B	6	★★	Occam's Razor
5.8	C	5	★★	Rhino Vista
5.10a	D	6	★★	Rhino Rave

☐ Occam's Razor_____ Date _____

☐ Rhino Vista_____ Date _____

☐ Rhino Rave _____ Date _____

Chris, reaching for gold, on
"Rhino Vista" - Hall Creek Rock p. (156)

5.8
A

Hall Creek Trestle

👁 69 p.154

Difficulty	Route	Bolts	Rating	Name
5.8	A	3	★	Erectile Dysfunction ❗ See #5 p. 159

☐ Erectile Dysfunction _____

_____ Date _____

Deception Route Warnings *Deception*

Most of the routes at the Deception are safe e.g. clean rock, no trails above walls, recently bolted, etc. Below is a list of the few routes that have additional safety considerations. Pay attention and you won't have to worry about stories you'll regret telling later.

#	Name	Warning
1	Overture & Underture 5.11a & 5.10c p. 143	Belay ledge is narrow. Be careful on first clip and use an auto-locking belay device if you have one.
2	Underground Economy 5.9 p. 144	Route starts below trestle. Belayer should back tie into bridge tie. Careful on the first clip or you'll slide down the face under the trestle.
3	Rat Face 5.10c p. 146	The top of the route is 40 meters so drag a rope or stop at chains mid route to rappel or lower. Loose rock at top of route.
4	The End 5.12a p. 146	Need two ropes to rappel from top of Rat Face route. Loose rocks at start. Loop a long sling around rock inside alcove for belay backup.
5	Erectile Dysfunction 5.9 p. 158	Miss the clip and slip on the first, second, or third bolt and you ground. And that will hurt.

Words of Wisdom

*Kindness and openness of mind
Will accomplish all goals:
Yours and those of others.*
   -*Tibetan Poem of Shabkar*

Best Deception Routes

For those of you who wish you could climb more but can't take more time off work because you owe too much, here are the routes you've got to climb before your job kills you.

Diff.	Name	Wall	Stats	
5.6	Homo Erectus p.125	Substation	☐ Lead ☐ Top Rope	☐ Redpoint ☐ Flash
	Mom There's Pink In My Burger p. 127	Write-Off Rock	☐ Lead ☐ Top Rope	☐ Redpoint ☐ Flash
5.7	Rug Monkey p. 125	Substation	☐ Lead ☐ Top Rope	☐ Redpoint ☐ Flash
	Glom Job p. 125	Substation	☐ Lead ☐ Top Rope	☐ Redpoint ☐ Flash
5.8	Rhino Vista p. 156	Hall Creek	☐ Lead ☐ Top Rope	☐ Redpoint ☐ Flash
	Glom Don p. 125	Substation	☐ Lead ☐ Top Rope	☐ Redpoint ☐ Flash
5.9	Absolutely Nothing p.153	We Did Rock	☐ Lead ☐ Top Rope	☐ Redpoint ☐ Flash
	Some Drugs p. 153	We Did Rock	☐ Lead ☐ Top Rope	☐ Redpoint ☐ Flash
5.10a	Won't Get Fooled Again p. 143	Deception	☐ Lead ☐ Top Rope	☐ Redpoint ☐ Flash
	Just Desert p.148	Deception	☐ Lead ☐ Top Rope	☐ Redpoint ☐ Flash
5.10b	You're Only Nice To Me When You're Wet p.123	Substation	☐ Lead ☐ Top Rope	☐ Redpoint ☐ Flash
	Subliminal p. 125	Substation	☐ Lead ☐ Top Rope	☐ Redpoint ☐ Flash
5.10c	Love Bucket p.136	Nevermind	☐ Lead ☐ Top Rope	☐ Redpoint ☐ Flash
	Slippery When Wet p. 123	Substation	☐ Lead ☐ Top Rope	☐ Redpoint ☐ Flash
5.10d	Big Mama p. 139	Nevermind	☐ Lead ☐ Top Rope	☐ Redpoint ☐ Flash
	Easily Amused p. 136	Nevermind	☐ Lead ☐ Top Rope	☐ Redpoint ☐ Flash
5.11a	The Overture p. 143	Deception	☐ Lead ☐ Top Rope	☐ Redpoint ☐ Flash
	Architect Rally p. 139	Nevermind	☐ Lead ☐ Top Rope	☐ Redpoint ☐ Flash

1/2 – 1 Day, Beginning Level (5.6 – 5.8)

Deception doesn't have a lot of beginner level climbs. In fact, in one afternoon you can get most of them done, and still have time for the exaggerated stories at the local pub.

Summary

Round Trip Time	4 hours from Seattle (assumes two climbers)
Hike	Easy – 8 minutes, .2 mile
Elevation Gain	200 feet
Best Season	Summer
Routes	Homo Erectus, Rug Monkey, Glom Dom, Mom There's Pink In My Burger, Bottoms Up
Notes	All the climbs are in the same general area so you'll be doing max climbing and minimum hiking.

Details

Directions	Page	Time
Drive to Deception parking area	118	35 min (from Seattle)
Hike to Substation Wall	120	8 min
Warm up on Homo Erectus (5.6)	125	40 min
Stay were you're at and climb Rug Monkey, just to the right of Homo Erectus (5.7)	125	40 min
Saunter 12 paces to the right (were the rock meets the concrete) and do Glom Don. (5.8)	125	40 min
Continue up the trail 20 meters and into the light on the Iron Horse trail to Write-Off Rock.	126	1 min
"Mom There's Pink In My Burger" on the right side of Write-Off Rock is next. (5.6)	127	40 min
Finish the fun on the route just to the right, "Bottoms Up". (5.7)	127	40 min
Hike back to parking area	118	7 min
Head down to the local North Bend Tavern and do "Bottoms Up" one more time.	---	---

1/2 – 1 Day, Intermediate Level (5.9 – 5.10c)

Great intermediate routes are scattered throughout the Deception area. Move quick and you can climb them all in an afternoon.

Summary

Round Trip Time	4 hours from Seattle
Hike	Easy – 8 minutes, .2 mile
Elevation Gain	200 feet
Best Season	Summer
Routes	Absolutely Nothing, Some Drugs, Blockhead, Just Dessert, Love Bucket
Notes	The best intermediate routes are scattered around Deception so you'll need to move quick to get'em in.

Details

Directions	Page	Time
Drive to the Deception parking area	118	35 min (from Seattle)
Hike up the main trail to We Did Rock wall.	153	13 min
Start on the left of We Did Rock and climb "Absolutely Nothing". (5.9)	153	30 min
Step right and do, "Some Drugs" (5.9).	153	30 min
Step right one more time and climb "Blockhead" (5.9).	153	30 min
Hike back down the Iron Horse trail and take the left side trail, at the end of the bridge, to the upper left section of Deception Wall.	148	7 min
Take your time and enjoy "Just Dessert" (5.10a)	148	35 min
Hike back down the side trail and turn left on the Iron Horse Trail to the Nevermind side trail.	131	5 min
Hike to Nevermind wall and see what you have left on the "Love Bucket" (5.10c).	136	40 min
Hike back to parking area	118	7 min
Wonder why you couldn't climb "Love Bucket"	---	----

Deception Itineraries Deception

1/2 – 1 Day, Advanced Level (5.10d – 5.12c)

The wall at Deception for big boys and girls is Nevermind.

Summary

Round Trip Time	4½ hours from Seattle
Hike	Easy – 10 minutes, .3 mile
Elevation Gain	200 feet
Best Season	Summer
Routes	Love Bucket, Easily Amused, Architect Rally, Canine Patrol, Culture Shock,
Notes	All single pitch routes, most thin vertical crimpers.

Details

Directions	Page	Time
Drive, or hitch hike, to Deception parking area.	118	35 min (from Seattle)
Hike up the main trail to the Iron Horse trail, turn left. Take the side trail right just after you cross the Trestle bridge to Nevermind Wall.	131	13 min
Get the blood flowing on "Love Bucket" (5.10c)	136	40 min
Step to the right and start it up on "Easily Amused" (5.10d)	136	40 min
Reload and go for "Architect Rally" (5.11a)	139	40 min
Take 10 then cruise up "Canine Patrol" (5.11c)	139	40 min
Reload and finish it on "Culture Shock" (5.12a)	140	40 min
Stumble back to the parking area.	118	11 min
Call the North Bend Tavorn and have them setup some recovery drinks.	---	---

Deception Route Listing

Diff	Route Name		Wall
5.4	☐ ★★ Bu The Rabbit	p. 127	Write-Off Rock
5.5	☐ ★★ Flammable Pajamas	p. 127	Write-Off Rock
5.6	☐ ★★★ Homo Erectus	p. 125	Substation
	☐ ★★ Mom There's Pink..	p. 127	Write-Off Rock
	☐ ★★ Easy Street	p. 150	We Did Rock
5.7	☐ ★★★ Rug Monkey	p. 125	Substation
	☐ ★★★ Glom Job	p. 125	Substation
	☐ ★★ Bottoms Up	p. 127	Write-Off Rock
	☐ ★★ Jiffy Pop	p. 146	Deception
	☐ ★★ Turf Safari	p. 121	Substation
	☐ ★ Your Sister	p. 150	We Did Rock
5.8	☐ ★★ Glob Don	p. 125	Substation
	☐ ★★ Rhino Vista	p. 156	Hall Rock
	☐ ★ Erectile Dysfunction	p. 158	Hall Creek
5.9	☐ ★★★★ Absolutely…	p. 153	We Did Rock
	☐ ★★★ Hurly-Burly	p. 125	Substation
	☐ ★★★ Some Drugs	p. 153	We Did Rock
	☐ ★★★ Blockhead	p. 153	We Did Rock
	☐ ★★ Underground…	p. 144	Deception Wall
	☐ ★★ Primordial Blues	p. 125	Substation
	☐ ★★ Knife In The…	p. 127	Write-Off Rock
	☐ ★★ Black Caboose	p. 153	We Did Rock
	☐ ★★ Strip Clip	p. 139	Nevermind
	☐ ★★ Occam's Razor	p. 156	Hall Rock
	☐ ★★ Sobriety	p. 153	We Did Rock

Diff	Route Name		Wall
5.10a	☐ ★★★★ Just Desert	p. 148	Deception
	☐ ★★★ Lovey-Dovey	p. 123	Substation
	☐ ★★★ Won't Get…	p. 143	Deception
	☐ ★★★ Neverigine	p. 135	Nevermind
	☐ ★★ Rhino Rave	p. 156	Hall Rock
	☐ ★ My X Wife…	p. 150	We Did Rock
5.10b	☐ ★★ Subliminal	p. 125	Substation
	☐ ★ Bwana Be Your Man	p. 121	Substation
	☐ ★ Strip Clip (Direct)	p. 139	Nevermind
5.10c	☐ ★★★ Love Bucket	p. 136	Nevermind
	☐ ★★★ The Underture	p. 143	Substation
	☐ ★★ Slippery When Wet	p. 123	Substation
	☐ ★★ Powerless	p. 135	Nevermind
	☐ ★★ Rat Face	p. 146	Deception
	☐ ★★ Chain Smoken	p. 125	Substation
	☐ ★★ Namby-Pamby	p. 123	Substation
	☐ ★ Side Dish	p. 148	Deception
	☐ ★ The Joke	p. 150	We Did Rock
	☐ ★ Sport Sickness	p. 155	Hall Rock
5.10d	☐ ★★★ Big Mama	p. 139	Nevermind
	☐ ★★★ Easily Amused	p. 136	Nevermind
	☐ ★★ Subversive	p. 125	Substation
	☐ ★★ You're Only Nice…	p. 123	Substation
	☐ ★★ You're Only Nice…	p. 123	Substation

5.11a	☐ ★ ★ ★ Hangover Helper	p. 123	Substation
	☐ ★ ★ ★ Late For Dinner	p. 148	Deception
	☐ ★ ★ ★ Steep Street	p. 132	Nevermind
	☐ ★ ★ ★ The Overture	p. 143	Deception
	☐ ★ ★ ★ Architect Rally	p. 139	Nevermind
5.11b	☐ ★ ★ ★ Negatherion	p. 135	Nevermind
	☐ ★ Easy Money	p. 129	Kiosk
5.11c	☐ ★ ★ Canine Patrol	p. 139	Nevermind
	☐ ★ ★ Hangerville	p. 135	Nevermind
5.11d	☐ ★ ★ ★ Rude Road	p. 132	Nevermind
	☐ ★ ★ Corporeal…	p. 135	Nevermind
5.12a	☐ ★ ★ Culture Shock	p. 140	Nevermind
	☐ ★ ★ Under Arrest	p. 132	Nevermind
	☐ ★ ★ The End	p. 146	Deception
	☐ ★ Stick Boy	p. 121	Substation
5.12b	☐ ★ ★ The Goblet	p. 140	Nevermind
5.13b	☐ ★ Deliverance	p. 142	Deception
5.13d	☐ ★ Open Project	p. 142	Deception

Words of Wisdom

Never give up on a dream because of the time it will take to accomplish it. The time will pass anyway.   *-Unknown*

Mt Washington

The Mt Washington climbing area offers some of the finest sport climbs in the North Bend area. Much of it is more remote and takes longer to access, but is less crowded than the Trestle area and has some grand views of the Snoqualmie valley. The lower crags, especially Amazonia and The Actual Cave, are subject to early season drippage (into June). The upper walls are blanketed with snow in the winter which usually melts off in April or May.

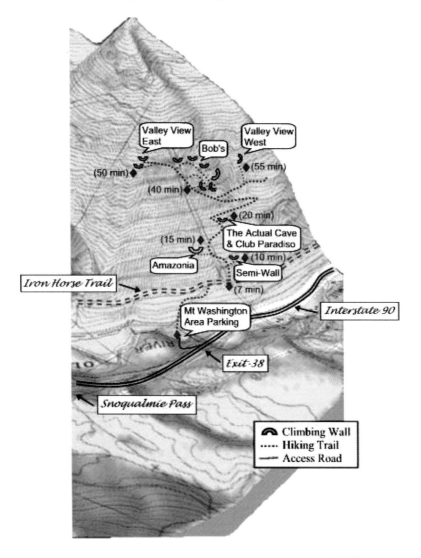

Mt Washington Statistics

Area Summary

Area	Height (Meters)	Number of Routes	Hiking Time (Minutes)	Elev. Gain (Feet)
Semi	15	4	10	300
Amazonia	20	15	15	400
Actual Cave	10	8	20	450
Club Paradiso	15	4	20	450
Chainsaw	15	6	45	1350
Peannacle	10	14	50	1400
Lost Resort	20	9	50	1400
Alpinia	15	4	55	1450
Presto Palace	10	1	55	1450
Slumbersome Ridge	15	8	60	1500
The Stien	10	1	65	1400
Valley View East	15	3	50	1350
Valley View West	25	8	55	1600

Elevation Profile

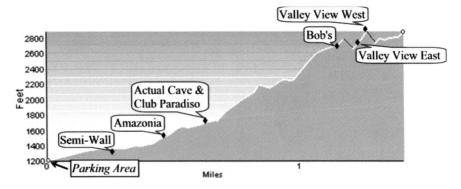

Wall Difficulty

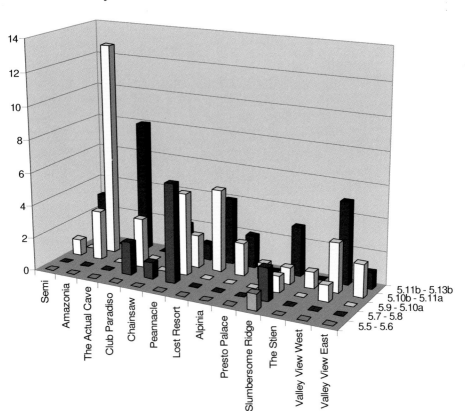

To get to the Mt Washington parking area, following Interstate I-90 (from Seattle or Snoqualmie Pass) and take Exit-38.

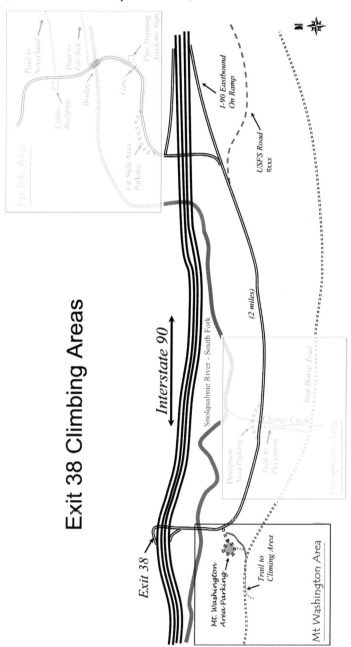

Exit 38 Climbing Areas

Getting to Mt Washington *Mt Washington*

If you're coming from the Seattle area (eastbound), take the first right a hundred meters after exiting the freeway at the Mt Washington / Twin Falls sign. Follow the dirt road up a gradual hill for 150 meters to the large parking area.

If you're coming from Snoqualmie pass, (westbound), turn left at the bottom of the Exit-38 off-ramp. Cross under I-90 and follow the paved road for 2 miles to the dirt road, just before a right corner which leads back to I-90. Follow the dirt road up a gradual hill for 150 meters to the large parking area.

Words Of Wisdom

What lies behind us and what lies before us are tiny maters compared to what lies within us.   *-Ralph Waldo Emerson*

Parking at Mt Washington

The parking area provides access to several state parks and also the climbing walls in the Mt Washington Area. The two state parks are Twin Falls and Iron Horse. Check http://www.parks.wa.gov for more information.

Washington State Parks requires a daily or annual fee for vehicle parking. Until 2008, the daily permit fee is $5 or $50 for an annual permit. The daily fee can be paid at the trail head. In 2008 the daily fee will increase to $7 and the annual fee will increase to $70. http://www.parks.wa.gov/parking/ has more information on purchasing annual permits. Note: Since the State implemented pay for parking at public parks, usage has dropped 30-70%. Go figure.

Enjoy this parking area because it's one of the best of any climbing area in the state. It has a lot of space, a new toilet, and an informative bulletin board, but, no latte stand. Note: Vandalism is always a concern at any trail head parking area so take your valuables with you or rig your vehicle to blow up if someone tries to break into it.

Weight Loss Closet

Trailhead to Mt Washington Climbing Area (& Twin Falls)

Parking

Hiking Trail to Mt Washington

To reach the Mt Washington area climbs, take the Twin Falls / Iron Horse trail from the parking area up a short hill to the Iron Horse Trail (more like a road) and veer right.

At ¼ mile (7 minute hike) turn left off the Iron Horse trail onto the Mt Washington trail. There aren't any signs or markers but it's easy to find given it's the first side trail on the left from the parking lot off the Iron Horse Trail.

Semi-Wall is the first climbing wall you'll come to on the Mt Washington Trail. As the name implies, it's a small wall with a few short routes on a steep side hill. It has the unfortunate honor of being the least climbed wall in the Mt Washington Area. It's not because the routes are bad but more so because its access trail is superbly camouflaged.

One of the enjoyable things about Semi-Wall is the access or side trail. It's a classic Northwest class IV vegetation scramble. When I first started climbing in the area, I remember thrashing around in search of the side trail. When I did finally stumble across it I spent several minutes getting even with the shrubbery and making sure the side trail would be more obvious. Two weeks later I brought a friend back to do a climb on the wall and I couldn't find the trail. Ya gotta love the Northwest.

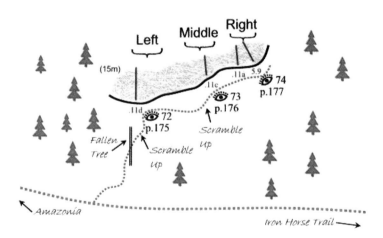

Semi-Wall

Tech Tip

Regular hiking shoes work okay for young children who want to climb, but better yet are aqua socks. –Lisa Lathe

The trick to finding Semi-Wall is locating the following clues.

First, find an old, but impressive, log/mud slide. The slide is about a 2 minute hike from the Mt Washington trail turnoff just after the trail switches back to the left.

The side trail turnoff to Semi-Wall is about 50 meters past the log slide on the right. If you pass over a creek you've gone too far.

5.11d
A

Main
Trail

👁 72 p.173

Difficulty	Route	Bolts	Rating	Route Name
5.11d	A	7	★ ★	Semi-Consciousness

☐ Semi-Consciousness _____ Date _____

5.11c
B

👁 73 p.173

☐ Semi-Automatic_____

_____

_____

_____

_____

_____

_____

_____

_____

_____

_____

_____

_____

_____

_____

_____

_____

_____

_____

_____

_____

_____

_____

_____ Date _____

Difficulty	Route	Bolts	Rating	Route Name	
5.11c	B	4	★★	Semi-Automatic	❗ See #1 p.239

☐ Semi-Suite _____

_____

_____

_____

_____

_____

_____

_____

Date _____

☐ Semi-Tough _____

_____

_____

_____

_____

_____

_____

_____

Date _____

👁 74 p.173

Difficulty	Route	Bolts	Rating	Route Name
5.11a	C	4	★	Semi-Suite
5.9	D	3	★	Semi-Tough

Amazonia is the best intermediate (5.10a - 5.11a) wall in the Mt. Washington Area. The face is 20 meters high, slightly inverted, and has absurdly consistent holds. There are 15 worthy routes on the wall so even if a few climbers beat you to the rock there's always something good to climb.

The interesting thing about the wall is that sunlight never touches it given it is North-facing and surrounded by dense forest. This makes it ideal in the middle of summer when the other walls are heating up. It's actually climbable in the winter because it's low enough in elevation to avoid snow and is slightly overhung, which keeps it mostly dry.

A unique thing about Amazonia is its built in shower or, as others have told me, a waterfall. The shower is in the middle of the wall and is present year around, albeit a bit more present during the winter. So, don't bother rushing home to clean yourself up after a day of experimenting with gravity. Simply use the built in shower and be ready to hit the town when you get back to the car.

Amazonia

The Amazonia wall is just to the left off the main Mt Washington trail a light 20 minute hike from the parking area. Look for an old steel logging cable embedded in the Mt Washington trail. Just to the left of it is the side trail to Amazonia. Follow the side trail for 20 meters and you'll be standing at the lower left corner of the wall.

Wet
Area

5.10d
A

5.10b
E

5.10a
D

5.11a
C

5.10c
B

75 p.178

Amazonia - Left

Difficulty	Route	Bolts	Rating	Name
5.10d	A	9	★★★	Arbo-Reality
5.10c	B	7	★★★★	Tropicana
5.11a	C	6	★★★★	Primus
5.10a	D	7	★★★★	Iguanarama
5.10b	E	6	★★★	Laceration of the Soul

☐ Arbo-Reality _____

_____ Date _____

☐ Tropicana _____

_____ Date _____

☐ Primus _____

_____ Date _____

☐ Iguanarama _____

_____ Date _____

☐ Laceration of the Soul _____

_____ Date _____

Mt Washington - 181

76 p.178

Amazonia - Middle

Mt Washington

Difficulty	Route	Bolts	Rating	Name
5.10b	E	6	★★★	Laceration of the Soul
5.10d	F	6	★★	Paste Human
5.11a	G	4	★★	Drier Adhesive To The ...
5.10b	H	6	★★★	Radioactive Decay
5.10b	I	6	★★★★	I Remember Drooling

☐ Laceration of the Soul _____

_____ Date _____

☐ Paste Human _____

_____ Date _____

☐ Drier Adhesive To The ... _____

_____ Date _____

☐ Radioactive Decay _____

_____ Date _____

☐ I Remember Drooling _____

_____ Date _____

5.10c
N

5.10d
O

5.10a
M

5.10d
L

5.9
K

5.10c
J

5.10b
I

77 p.178

Amazonia – Right

Difficulty	Route	Bolts	Rating	Name	
5.10b	I	6	★★★★	I Remember Drooling	
5.10c	J	6	★★★	Scrubbing Neon	
5.9	K	4	★★★	Sodflesh	! See #3 p. 239
5.10d	L	4	★★	Firewalk On Me	
5.10a	M	3	★★	Q.D. Pie	
5.10c	N	3	★★	Ten-ish Ooze	
5.10d	O	2	★	Enema	

☐ I Remember Drooling _____

_____ Date _____

☐ Scrubbing Neon _____ _____

_____ Date _____

☐ Sodflesh _____

_____ Date _____

☐ Firewalk On Me _____ _____

_____ Date _____

☐ Ten-ish Ooze _____

_____ Date _____

☐ Q.D. Pie _____ _____

_____ Date _____

☐ Enema _____ _____

_____ Date _____

Drew, wondering about his belayer, on
"I Remember Drooling" – 5.10b (p.184)

Although Club Paradiso and The Actual Cave are part of the same wall, the climbing couldn't be more different. At the Club you'll find big, reassuring holds on a vertical face. Next door at the Cave you'll find the same type of holds but inverted to 90 degrees past vertical i.e. overhanging.

Club Paradiso is the wettest wall in the area as water indiscriminately drains over it most of the year. August and September are usually the only months it's dry, and even then it looks wet because it's covered in black lichen.

The Actual Cave is... well an actual cave. It's one of the best in the Snoqualmie Valley for some real inverted climbing fun. Your climbing skills had better be razor-sharp because the routes start in the mid 5.11's and crank up into 5.13's.

The Actual Cave & Club Paradiso

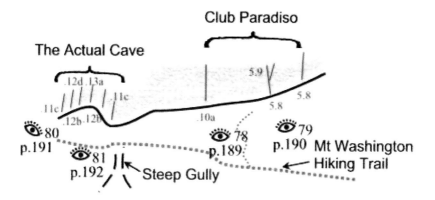

Club Paradiso and The Actual Cave are a 25 minute hike from the parking lot or a 5 minute hike past Amazonia Wall. They're practically part of the Mt Washington trail so, unless you're hiking with a blindfold, you can't miss them.

The Cave

5.10a
A

Main Trail

78 p.187

Difficulty	Route	Bolts	Rating	Name
5.10a	A	7	★★★	Trappline

79 p.187

Difficulty	Route	Bolts	Rating	Name
5.8	B	7	★★★	Lush
5.9	C	8	★★★	Luscious
5.8	D	7	★★	Just Because You're Paranoid…

☐ Lush _____ Date _____

☐ Luscious _____ Date _____

☐ Just Because You're Paranoid Doesn't Mean They're Not After You____ Date _____

The Actual Cave - Left

XX
XX

5.11c
A

5.12b
B

Mt Washington
Hiking Trail

👁 80 p.187

Difficulty	Route	Bolts	Rating	Name
5.11c	A	4	★★★	100% Beef
5.12b	B	4	★★	Bikini Girls With Turbo Drills ❗ See #7 p. 239

☐ 100% Beef _____ Date _____

☐ Bikini Girls with Turbo Drills _____ Date _____

81 p.187

The Actual Cave - Right

Difficulty	Route	Bolts	Rating	Name
5.12d	C	7	★	Positive Vibrations
5.13a	D	7	★★★	Acid Rock
5.12d	E	9	★	Spartacus
5.12b	F	8	★★	Cyanide
5.11c	G	5	★★★★	Giant
5.12a	H	7	★★★	Mr. Big

□ Positive Vibrations _____ Date _____

_____

□ Acid Rock _____ Date _____

_____

□ Spartacus _____ Date _____

_____

□ Cyanide_____ Date _____

_____

□ Giant_____ Date _____

_____

□ Mr. Big _____ Date _____

_____

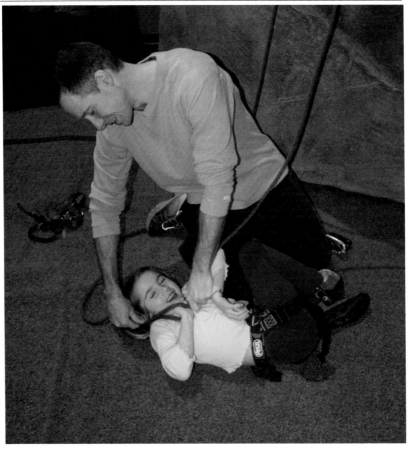

Author and daughter, Ellie, taking a climbing break.
Photo by Mikaila Fulfs

Words of Wisdom

The highest reward for a man's toils is not what he gets for it
but what he becomes by it.   *-John Ruskain*

Simply put, Bob's area offers some of the best overall sport climbing in the area. It has over 50 high quality beginner to advanced routes and, because it's high on the scenic shoulder of Mt Washington, it has great views of the valley. This combination makes for a nice afternoon of climbing and relaxing in the mountains.

Although Bob offers some great climbing, it gets far fewer climbers than Deception or Far Side. It's primarily because routes at Deception and Far Side are a short, easy hike compared to almost an hour of moderate hiking for Bob's area.

Note: Bob's area is just under 3000 feet elevation and is usually covered with several inches of snow during the winter.

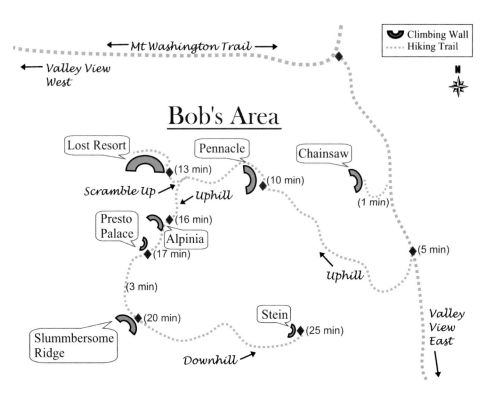

Getting to Bob's Area

Follow the Mt Washington trail for 2 miles from the parking lot (50 minute hike) until you reach a major fork in the trail (see picture below). The left trail leads to Bob's area and Valley View East. The right trail is the continuation of the Mt Washington trail and the Valley View West Wall.

Chainsaw Wall is the first of a series of rock shelves on the Northern ridge of Mt Washington. It's a great little wall that has a lot to be proud of. It's quick and easy to locate, has excellent routes, is nicely exposed, and has open views of the valley. It also has one of only three crack routes in the area that requires gear.

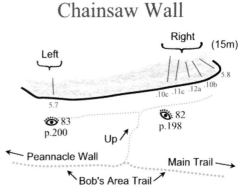

To reach Chainsaw Wall, take the first side trail to the right (about a three minute hike) after leaving the main Mt Washington Trail. The side trail is about 50 meters long and ascends a short side hill to a ledge at the base of the wall. See map on page 195 for more reference.

Chainsaw Wall - Right

Difficulty	Route	Bolts	Rating	Name
5.10c	A	5	★★★★	Posthumous Joy and Elation
5.11c	B	5	★★★	My Evil Plan
5.12a	C	5	★★★★	Stihl Fingers
5.10b	D	5	★★★	Texas Chainsaw Cheerleaders
5.8	E	5	★★	Chainsaw Chalupa

☐ Posthumous Joy and Elation _____

_____ Date _____

☐ My Evil Plan _____ _____

_____ Date _____

☐ Stihl Fingers _____

_____ Date _____

☐ Texas Chainsaw Cheerleaders _____

_____ Date _____

☐ Chainsaw Chalupa _____

_____ Date _____

83 p.197

Difficulty	Route	Bolts	Rating	Name
5.7	A	Pro to 1 ½ "	★	Crack One With Me

□ Crack One With Me _____ Date _____

Right - Martha and Steven, enjoying the day,
on "*A Summer Known As Fall*" - 5.8 (p.205)

Peannacle wall is the most popular wall in Bob's area. The main reason – a heap of 5.8-5.9 routes on an outstanding wedge of very solid, highly textured rock protruding north into the valley. Without a doubt it's the best place to visit, climb hard, then kick back and enjoy a lunch, some sun, and scenery.

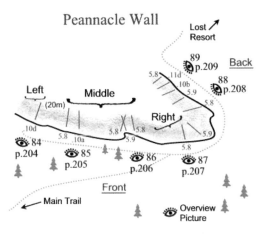

To reach Peannacle Wall, first follow the direction to Bob's Area (p. 196).

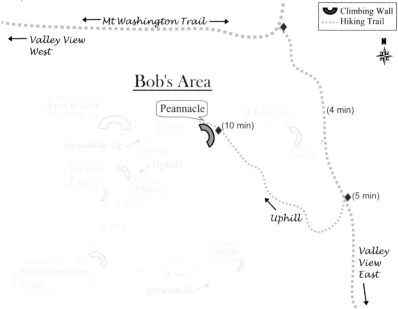

Bob's Area

From the turn-off of Mt. Washington trail, follow Bob's Area side trail for 4 minutes, to the second side trail to the right (first side trail leads to Chainsaw). The trail angles up a short hill, about a four minute hike, to the front, eastern section of Peannacle.

5.10d
A

👁 84 p.202

Difficulty	Route	Bolts	Rating	Name
5.10d	A	3	★ ★	What Does Bob Want?

☐ What Does Bob Want?_____ Date _____

Difficulty	Route	Bolts	Rating	Name
5.8	B	8	★★★	A Summer Known as Fall
5.10a	C	6	★★★	Gallivant

☐ A Summer Known as Fall _____ Date _____

☐ Gallivant _____ Date _____

86 p.202

Difficulty	Route	Bolts	Rating	Name
5.8	D	Pro to 2"	★	Salutiferous Exaltation… ❗ See #2 p. 239
5.9	E	5	★★★	Killer Bob
5.8	F	3	★★	The Owl

☐ Salutiferous Exaltation… _____ Date _____

☐ Killer Bob _____ Date _____

☐ The Owl _____ Date _____

87 p.202

Difficulty	Route	Bolts	Rating	Name
5.8	G	3	★★★	Peanut Brittle
5.9	H	3	★★★	Never Was A Cowgirl

☐ Peanut Brittle _____ Date _____

☐ Never Was A Cowgirl _____ Date _____

Peannacle Wall - Back Left

Difficulty	Route	Bolts	Rating	Name
5.8	I	5	★★★	A Castle So Crystal Clear
5.9	J	7	★★★	Awannaduya

☐ A Castle So Crystal Clear_____ Date _____

☐ Awannaduya _____ Date _____

Difficulty	Route	Bolts	Rating	Name
5.9	J	7	★★★	Awannaduya
5.10b	K	1 Pro to 3"	★★★	One Chance Out Between Two Worlds
5.11d	L	6	★★	The Magician Longs To See
5.8	M	4	★★	Through The Darkness Of Future's Past

☐ Awannaduya _____ Date _____

☐ One Chance Out Between Two Worlds _____ Date _____

☐ The Magician Longs To See_____ Date _____

☐ Through The Darkness Of Future's Past _____ Date _____

Tina, on the edge, on
"Gallivant" – 5.10a (p. 205)

Lost Resort Wall is the largest wall in Bob's area. The pitches are full on, sustained climbing on amazingly consistent edges. The only thing this wall lacks is sun. Trees crowd the bottom of the wall and grow to nearly its height, cleverly hiding it. So, if you're a 5.13 wanna be climber (but still climb mostly 5.11's) then this wall is a must visit.

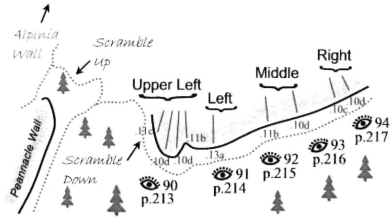

Lost Resort Wall

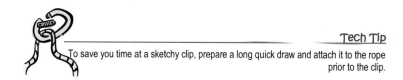

Tech Tip

To save you time at a sketchy clip, prepare a long quick draw and attach it to the rope prior to the clip.

To reach the Lost Resort wall, follow the hiking trail for 20 meters around the back side of Peannacle wall to a trail fork.

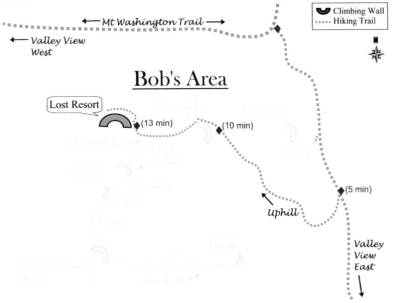

The right fork leads to Lost Resort wall. The left trail is a short, but steep, scramble to the top of Peannacle Point and continues to the upper walls Alpinia, Presto, Slumbersome, and The Stein.

Difficulty	Route	Bolts	Rating	Name
5.11c	A	5	★★★	Give Your Shelf To Me
5.10d	B	6	★★★★	Andante Favori
5.10d	C	8	★★★★	Appassionata
5.11b	D	9	★★★★	Crescendo Of The Sarcophagus Bleeding

☐ Give Your Shelf To Me _____ Date _____

☐ Andante Favori _____ Date _____

☐ Appassionata _____ Date _____

☐ Crescendo Of The Sarcophagus Bleeding _____ Date _____

Lost Resort - Left

5.11b
D

👁 91 p.211

5.13a
E

Difficulty	Route	Bolts	Rating	Name
5.11b	D	9	★★★★	Crescendo Of The Sarcophagus Bleeding
5.13a	E	10	★★★	Crawling From The Wreckage

☐ Crescendo Of The Sarcophagus Bleeding _____ Date _____

☐ Crawling From The Wreckage_____ _____ Date _____

5.11d
F

👁 92 p.211

Difficulty	Route	Bolts	Rating	Name
5.11d	F	6	★★★	Liberty Smack

☐ Liberty Smack_____ Date _____

93 p.211

Difficulty	Route	Bolts	Rating	Name
5.10d	G	7	★ ★	Satoric Inclination

☐ Satoric Inclination_____ Date _____

94 p.211

Difficulty	Route	Bolts	Rating	Name
5.10c	H	8	★★★★	Firing Up Bob
5.10d	I	7	★★★	POSTINSANGUIFI...

☐ Firing Up Bob _____ Date _____

☐ POSTINSAN... _____ Date _____

Alpinia & Presto Palace

Alpinia wall is Peannacle wall's little brother. It's a smaller shelf of rock on the ridge line above Peannacle. Like its bigger brother, it also has nice views of the valley. Most of the routes are mid 5.11 and all are well worth the extra couple minutes hiking time required to reach them.

Presto Palace is a small edge of rock about 10 meters high just around the corner from Alpinia. It has one lonely 5.11a route that angles left on a slightly inclined face with meager holds. "Presto Condo" or "Presto Play House" would have been a more appropriate name.

Alpinia & Presto Palace

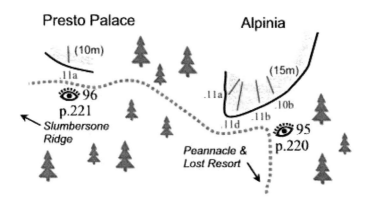

√ It Out

Along the ridge are robust groups of ferns, Polystichum Munitum (Western Sword Fern). It is the most common fern in the area. The bumps under the leaf are its spores, aka seeds, to ensure there is a next generation.

Alpinia wall is directly above Peannacle wall on the continued ridge line. The easiest way to access it is via the trail around Peannacle.

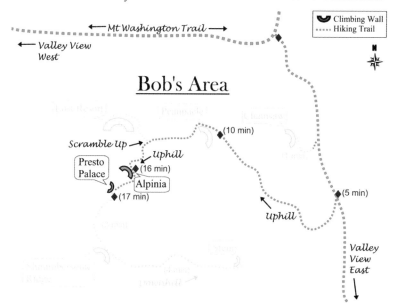

Follow the trail up a short scramble to the top of Peannacle and veer right up the ridge on a short trail (about 100 meters or 2 minute hike) to Alpinia. The trail continues left around the base of Alpinia and leads to Presto Palace.

95 p.218

Difficulty	Route	Bolts	Rating	Name
5.11a	A	4	★★★	Aperture Ecstasy In A Nocturne Divine
5.11d	B	6	★★★	Inverted Rain Ascending
5.11b	C	5	★★★	Green Buddha
5.10b	D	6	★★	El Astronato

☐ Aperture Ecstasy In A Nocturne Divine _____ Date _____

☐ Inverted Rain Ascending _____ Date _____

☐ Green Buddha _____ Date _____

☐ El Astronato _____ Date _____

Presto Palace

5.11a
A

Alpinia

Slumbersome

👁 96 p.218

Difficulty	Route	Bolts	Rating	Name
5.11a	A	4	★★	Salterello Presto

☐ Salterello Presto _____ Date _____

Slumbersome Ridge is a sweet wall for all levels of climbers. Its unique combination of slightly overhung faces with gentle slab sides offers a full range of climbing difficulty from 5.6 to 5.11a. If you're just getting started in the climbing business and the easier routes on Peannacle are crowded, saunter up the ridge to Slumbersome - you won't be disappointed.

The Stein is a cute little rock crag just down the ridge with a single route to its name. Much like Presto Palace, it doesn't get climbed a lot, so be prepared for some vegetation management to access the route.

The Stein & Slumbersome Ridge

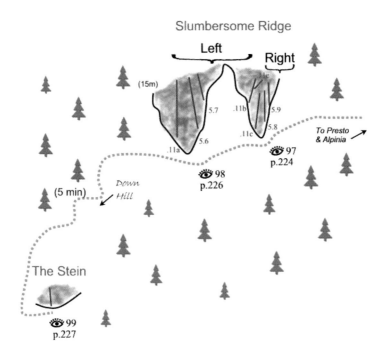

Slumbersome Ridge and The Stein are the last of the upper walls in Bob's area. The easiest way to reach Slumbersome is to follow the Peannacle Wall side trail around Peannacle and up the ridge past Alpinia and Presto. The Stein is about 70 meters across and down the ridge trail, from Slummbersome, on your left.

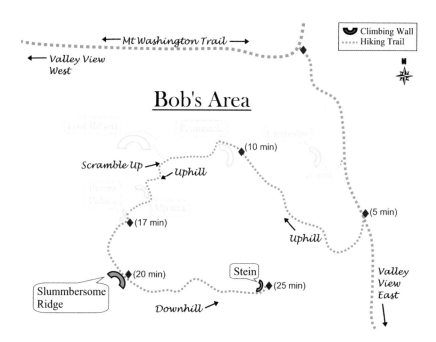

97 p. 222

Slumbersome Ridge - Left

Mt Washington

Difficulty	Route	Bolts	Rating	Name
5.11a	A	7	★★	To Crest In Violent Slumber
5.6	B	8	★★★	Slumbersome Ridge
5.7	C	4	★★★	Autumnal Equinox
5.11b	D	8	★★	Stemming Out Beyond The Grey
5.11c	E	8	★★★	The Validity Of Foreverness Twisted …
5.11c	F	4	★★	Imbibing Knowledge From A Mortal Furnace

☐ To Crest In Violent Slumber _____ Date _____

☐ Slumbersome Ridge_____ Date _____

☐ Autumnal Equinox _____ Date _____

☐ Stemming Out Beyond The Grey _____ Date _____

☐ The Validity Of Foreverness Twisted … _____ Date _____

☐ Imbibing Knowledge From a Mortal Furnace _____ Date _____

98 p.222

Difficulty	Route	Bolts	Rating	Name
5.8	G	3 (Pro to 2")	★★★	Ultra-Mega Crack
5.9	H	8	★★★	Ultra-Mega Slab

☐ Ultra-Mega Crack _____ Date _____

☐ Ultra-Mega Slab _____ Date _____

The Stein

99 p.222

Difficulty	Route	Bolts	Rating	Name
5.10d	A	6	★★★	You'll Only Get Spanked If It's Wet

☐ You'll Only Get Spanked If It's Wet _____ Date _____

Mt Washington - 227

Valley View East

Mt Washington

Valley View East is a couple of crags an easy ten minute hike past Bob's area. There are two routes on the lower crag and one on the upper. Much like Peannacle Point and Alpinia, the crags are on a ridge that overlooks the Snoqualmie valley.

On warm summer weekends you will almost always find happy harnessed people playing on Amazonia and Peannacle but not so for Valley View East. It generally only gets half a dozen visitors a year. So, if you're looking for some climbing without other happy harnessed people, head over to Valley View East.

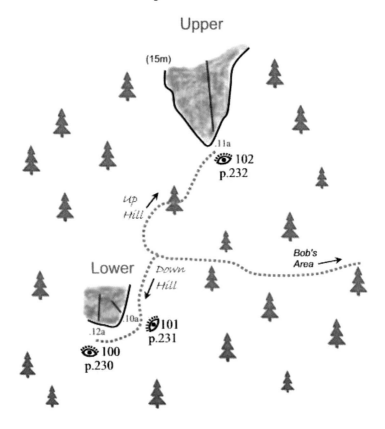

Valley View East

To reach Valley View East, continue on the Bob's area trail past the Peannacle Point and The Stein side trails ¼ mile (about a 10 minute hike) on an old logging road/trail.

The trail leads to the middle of the upper and lower crag. The left fork leads down a short hill to the base of the lower crag. The right trail fork leads up a short hill to the base of the upper crag.

Note: The trail may be overgrown given it doesn't get a lot of traffic. So, let your climbing partner go first and reassure them that it's bound to improve just around the next corner.

5.12a
A

100 p.228

Difficulty	Route	Bolts	Rating	Name
5.12a	A	7	★★★★	Passage

☐ Passage _____ Date _____

5.10b
B

101 p. 228

Difficulty	Route	Bolts	Rating	Name
5.10b	B	3	★★	Above the Mantle

☐ Above the Mantle _____ Date _____

5.11a
A

102 p. 228

Difficulty	Route	Bolts	Rating	Name
5.11a	A	4	★ ★ ★	Patience on the Edge of Beauty

☐ Patience on the Edge of Beauty _____ Date _____

Valley View West is one of the recent additions to the area and is destined to become one of the most popular. It's loaded with superbly crafted intermediate to advanced climbs and, at over 3000 feet elevation, it has the best views of any wall in the valley. On a clear day you can inspect Bellevue, Seattle, and even the Olympic Mountains.

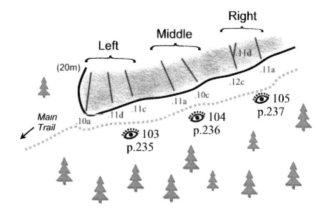

Valley View West

To reach Valley View West, continue past the side trail to Bob's area ¼ mile (6 minute hike) and look for an old uprooted tree stump on your left.

Continue past the old stump another 10 meters and you'll see a side trail on your left which goes up a short embankment. The side trail ascends the ridge about 200 meters to the base of the Valley View West Wall.

5.10a
A

5.11d
B

5.11c
C

👁 103 p.233

Difficulty	Route	Bolts	Rating	Name
5.10a	A	5	★★★★	Stairway to Heavin' ! See #4 p. 239
5.11d	B	8	★★★	My Sorrow Bleeds With Such Delight
5.11c	C	1 & Pro to 2 ½ "	★★★★	AtaxiCrack ! See #5 p. 239

☐ Stairway to Heavin' _____ Date _____

☐ My Sorrow Bleeds With Such Delight _____ Date _____

☐ AtaxiCrack _____ Date _____

5.11a
D

5.10c
E

👁 104 p.233

Difficulty	Route	Bolts	Rating	Name
5.11a	D	10	★★★	Traverse To The Hole
5.10c	E	9	★★	Rock Party Vagabond ❗ See #6 p. 239

☐ Traverse To The Hole _____ Date _____

☐ Rock Party Vagabond _____ Date _____

105 p.233

Difficulty	Route	Bolts	Rating	Name
5.12c	F	8	★★★	And Empty It Remains
5.12a	G	7	★★★★	Empty Martyr Breeding Room
5.11a	H	1 (Pro to 1½)	★★★	Cascadian Crack

☐ And Empty It Remains _____ Date _____

☐ Empty Martyr Breeding Room _____ Date _____

☐ Cascadian Crack _____ Date _____

Mel, assessing her options, on
"Stairway To Heavin"' – 5.10a (p.235)
Photo by Dave Argento

You need to pay attention on every route you climb, but here are the Mt. Washington routes that deserve some additional caution.

#	Name	Warning
1	Semi-Automatic 5.11c p. 176	Helpful to stickclip the first bolt. Also, the trail to the route crosses over a thin ledge.
2	Salutiferous Exaltation… 5.8 p. 206	A bit run out after crossing Killer Bob route.
3	Sodflesh 5.9 p. 185	Run out, but moderate climbing, to the first bolt.
4	Stairway to Heavin 5.10a p.235	Scramble up onto the large block to belay and begin the climb.
5	Ataxicrack 5.11c p. 235	Route is 30 meters so a sixty meter rope would be handy.
6	Rock Party Vegabond 5.10c p. 236	Using longer draws will help with rope drag about ¾ up the face where the route takes a left.
7	Bikini Girls With Turbo Drills 5.12b p. 191	Stick clip the beginning hangers and leave the crash pad at home.

_____ **Did Ya Know?**

Climbing harnesses are rated to withstand 10-16kn of force before they tear apart. Webbing, 12-16kn; Carabineers, 18-25kn; Spectra 24-28kn. The human body… 6-8kn.

For those of you who wish you could climb more but can't take more time off work because you owe too much, here are the routes you've got to climb before your job kills you.

Diff.	Name		Wall	Stats	
5.6	Slummbersome Ridge	p. 225	Slummbersome	☐ Lead ☐ Top Rope	☐ Redpoint ☐ Flash
5.7	Autumnal Equinox	p. 225	Slummbersome	☐ Lead ☐ Top Rope	☐ Redpoint ☐ Flash
5.8	A Castle So Crystal Clear	p.208	Peannacle	☐ Lead ☐ Top Rope	☐ Redpoint ☐ Flash
5.9	A Summer Known As Fall	p. 205	Peannacle	☐ Lead ☐ Top Rope	☐ Redpoint ☐ Flash
	Killer Bob	p. 206	Peannacle	☐ Lead ☐ Top Rope	☐ Redpoint ☐ Flash
	Sodflesh	p. 185	Amazonia	☐ Lead ☐ Top Rope	☐ Redpoint ☐ Flash
5.10a	Iguanarama	p. 181	Amazonia	☐ Lead ☐ Top Rope	☐ Redpoint ☐ Flash
	Stairway To Heavin'	p.235	Valley View West	☐ Lead ☐ Top Rope	☐ Redpoint ☐ Flash
5.10b	I Remember Drooling	p.185	Amazonia	☐ Lead ☐ Top Rope	☐ Redpoint ☐ Flash
	Laceration Of The Soul	p.181	Amazonia	☐ Lead ☐ Top Rope	☐ Redpoint ☐ Flash
5.10c	Tropicana	p. 181	Amazonia	☐ Lead ☐ Top Rope	☐ Redpoint ☐ Flash
	Firing Up Bob	p.217	Lost Resort	☐ Lead ☐ Top Rope	☐ Redpoint ☐ Flash
5.10d	Appassionata	p. 213	Lost Resort	☐ Lead ☐ Top Rope	☐ Redpoint ☐ Flash
	Andante Favori	p. 213	Lost Resort	☐ Lead ☐ Top Rope	☐ Redpoint ☐ Flash
5.11a	Primus	p. 181	Amazonia	☐ Lead ☐ Top Rope	☐ Redpoint ☐ Flash
	Aperture Ecstasy In A Nocturne Divine	p. 220	Alpinia	☐ Lead ☐ Top Rope	☐ Redpoint ☐ Flash
5.11b	Crescendo Of The Sarcophagus Bleeding	p. 214	Lost Resort	☐ Lead ☐ Top Rope	☐ Redpoint ☐ Flash
	Green Budda	p. 220	Alpinia	☐ Lead ☐ Top Rope	☐ Redpoint ☐ Flash

Mt Washington Itineraries

1/2 – 1 Day, Beginning Level (5.6 – 5.8)

There are very few beginning level routes on Mt Washington. So, if you're at the 5.6/5.7 level then you're better off heading to the Far Side or Deception areas.

Summary

Round Trip Time	5 ½ hours (round trip from Seattle)
Hike	Moderate – 50 minutes, 1.3 miles
Elevation Gain	1400 feet
Best Season	Summer
Routes	A Summer Known As Fall, The Owl, Peanut Brittle, A Castle So Crystal Clear, Through The Darkness of Futures Past
Notes	Nice alpine hike. Plan on spending most of the day. Don't forget to bring your lunch and your camera.

Details

Directions	Page	Time
Drive to the Mt Washington/Twin Falls parking area.	169	35 min
Follow the Twin Falls trail from the parking area to the Iron Horse trail and take the Mt Washington side trail to the left.	172	10 min
Follow the Mt Washington trail up the ridge to the side trail which leads to Bob's area.	196	35 min
Continue 100 meters on Bob's area trail to the Peannacle Wall side trail. Follow it to the wall.	202	5 min
Start on the front left side of Peannacle and climb "A Summer Known As Fall" (5.8)	205	30 min
Walk to the middle of the wall and spend some time with "The Owl" (5.8).	206	30 min
Step right and savor some "Peanut Brittlo" (5.8)	207	30 min
Walk around the back of Peannacle and find "A Castle So Crystal Clear" (5.8).	208	30 min
Finish up on the far right route "Through The Darkness Of Future's Past" (5.8).	209	30 min
Hike back to parking area	169	40 min

Mt Washington Itineraries

1/2 – 1 Day, Intermediate Level (5.9 – 5.10c)

The Mt Washington area has some sweet intermediate climbs, most of which are at Amazonia Wall.

Summary

Round Trip Time	5 hours (round trip from Seattle)
Hike	Moderate – 20 minutes, .6 mile
Elevation Gain	400 feet
Best Season	Summer
Routes	Sod Flesh, Iguanarama, Laceration Of The Soul, Radioactive Decay, I Remember Drooling, Tropicana
Notes	Amazonia Wall is the place for some great intermediate routes. Don't bother bringing sun screen.

Details

Directions	Page	Time
Get yourself to the Mt Washington parking area.	169	35 min
Follow the Mt Washington/Twin Falls trail from the parking area to the Iron Horse trail and take the Mt Washington side trail to the left.	172	10 min
Follow the Mt Washington trail to the Amazonia wall side trail.	179	30 min
Start on the right side of the wall and warm up on "Sod Flesh" (5.9)	185	30 min
Move to the left and wait in line on "Iguanarama" (5.10a).	181	30 min
Step right and do "Laceration Of The Soul", if it's dry (5.10b).	181	30 min
Next, feel the burn on "Radioactive Decay" (5.10b).	183	30 min
Go with the flow on "I Remember Drooling" (5.10b).	185	30 min
If you have anything left in the tank, spend some time on "Tropicana" (5.10c).	181	30 min
Skip back to parking area.	169	10 min
Stop at the grocery store and pickup a pain killer.	---	---

Mt Washington Itineraries

1/2 – 1 Day, Advanced Level (5.10d – 5.12c)

Mt Washington has two great places for advanced climbing: Lost Resort Wall and Valley View West. Since you're hiking for almost an hour to reach either place, you might as well end up in the sun at Valley View West.

Summary

Round Trip Time	6.0 hours from Seattle
Hike	Moderate – 3.5 miles (round trip)
Elevation Gain	1400 feet
Best Season	Summer
Routes	Stairway to Heavin, Traverse to the Hole, My Sorrow Bleeds With Such Delight, And Empty It Remains
Notes	Bring your rack and double the fun.

Details

Directions	Page	Time
Find the Mt Washington parking area at Exit 38.	169	35 min
Follow the Mt Washington/Twin Falls trail from the parking area to the Iron Horse trail and take the Mt Washington side trail to the left.	172	10 min
Continue up the Mt Washington trail to the Valley View West trail.	234	40 min
Follow the side trail up the ridge to the base of the Valley View West wall.	233	8 min
Start on the left side of the wall and warm up the mind and body on "Stairway to Heavin' (5.10a)	235	30 min
Move right to the middle of the wall and search for the meaning of "Traverse to the Hole" (5.11a).	236	30 min
Step back left and enjoy "My Sorrow Bleeds With Such Delight" (5.11d).	235	30 min
Cruise to the right side of the wall and crank it up one more time on "And Empty It Remains" (5.12c).	237	30 min
Just for fun, do the variation "Empty Martyr Breeding Room" (5.12a).	237	30 min
Hike back knowing you've done good work on the rock.	169	40 min

Mt Washington Route Listings

Diff.	Name		Wall
5.6	☐ ★ ★ ★ Slumbersome Ridge	p. 225	Slumbersome
5.7	☐ ★ ★ ★ Autumnal Equinox	p. 225	Slumbersome
	☐ ★ Crack One With Me	p. 200	Chainsaw
5.8	☐ ★ ★ ★ A Castle So Crystal Clear	p. 208	Peannacle
	☐ ★ ★ ★ A Summer Known As Fall	p. 205	Peannacle
	☐ ★ ★ ★ Lush	p. 190	Club Paradiso
	☐ ★ ★ ★ Ultra-Mega Crack	p. 226	Slumbersome
	☐ ★ ★ ★ Peanut Brittle	p. 207	Peannacle
	☐ ★ ★ Chainsaw Chalupa	p. 199	Chainsaw
	☐ ★ ★ The Owl	p. 206	Peannacle
	☐ ★ ★ Just Because You're...	p. 190	Club Paradiso
	☐ ★ ★ Through The ...	p. 209	Peannacle
	☐ ★ Salutiferous Exaltation...	p. 206	Peannacle
5.9	☐ ★ ★ ★ Luscious	p. 190	Club Paradiso
	☐ ★ ★ ★ Killer Bob	p. 206	Peannacle
	☐ ★ ★ ★ Sodflesh	p. 185	Amazonia
	☐ ★ ★ ★ Never Was A Cowgirl	p. 207	Peannacle
	☐ ★ ★ ★ Awannaduya	p. 209	Peannacle
	☐ ★ ★ ★ Ultra-Mega Slab	p. 226	Slumbersome
	☐ ★ Semi-Tough	p. 177	Semi-Wall
5.10a	☐ ★ ★ ★ ★ Iguanarama	p. 181	Amazonia
	☐ ★ ★ ★ ★ Stairway to Heavin'	p. 235	View West
	☐ ★ ★ ★ Trappline	p. 189	Club Paradiso
	☐ ★ ★ ★ Gallivant	p. 205	Peannacle
	☐ ★ ★ Q.D. Pie	p. 185	Amazonia
5.10b	☐ ★ ★ ★ ★ I Remember Drooling	p. 185	Amazonia
	☐ ★ ★ ★ Laceration of the Soul	p. 181	Amazonia
	☐ ★ ★ ★ Texas Chainsaw ...	p. 199	Chainsaw
	☐ ★ ★ ★ One Chance Out ...	p. 209	Peannacle
	☐ ★ ★ El Astronato	p. 220	Alpinia
	☐ ★ ★ Above The Mantle	p. 231	View East
	☐ ★ ★ ★ Radioactive Decay	p. 183	Amazonia
5.10c	☐ ★ ★ ★ ★ Tropicana	p. 181	Amazonia
	☐ ★ ★ ★ ★ Posthumous Joy ...	p. 199	Chainsaw
	☐ ★ ★ ★ ★ Firing Up Bob	p. 217	Lost Resort
	☐ ★ ★ ★ Scrubbing Neon	p. 185	Amazonia
	☐ ★ ★ Rock Party Vagabond	p. 236	View West
	☐ ★ ★ Ten-ish Ooze	p. 185	Amazonia
5.10d	☐ ★ ★ ★ ★ Appassionata	p. 213	Lost Resort
	☐ ★ ★ ★ ★ Andante Favori	p. 213	Lost Resort
	☐ ★ ★ ★ POSTINSANGUI...	p. 217	Lost Resort
	☐ ★ ★ ★ Satoric Inclination	p. 216	Lost Resort
	☐ ★ ★ ★ Arbo-Reality	p. 181	Amazonia
	☐ ★ ★ ★ You'll Only Get Spanked..	p. 227	The Stein
	☐ ★ ★ Paste Human	p. 183	Amazonia
	☐ ★ ★ Firewalk On Me	p. 185	Amazonia
	☐ ★ ★ What Does Bob Want?	p. 204	Peannacle
	☐ ★ Enema	p. 185	Amazonia

Mt Washington - 244

Mt Washington Route Listings

Diff.	Name		Wall	Diff.	Name		Wall
5.11a	☐ ★ ★ ★ ★ Primus	p. 181	Amazonia	5.11d	☐ ★ ★ ★ My Sorrow Bleeds...	p. 235	View West
	☐ ★ ★ ★ Aperture Ecstasy...	p. 220	Alpinia		☐ ★ ★ ★ Liberty Smack	p. 215	Lost Resort
	☐ ★ ★ ★ Traverse To The Hole	p. 236	View West		☐ ★ ★ ★ Inverted Rain Ascending	p. 220	Alpinia
	☐ ★ ★ ★ Patience On The Edge	p. 232	View East		☐ ★ ★ The Magician Longs To See	p. 209	Peannacle
	☐ ★ ★ ★ Cascadian Crack	p. 237	View West		☐ ★ Semian Consciousness	p. 175	Semi-Wall
	☐ ★ ★ Salterello Presto	p. 221	Presto Palace	5.12a	☐ ★ ★ ★ ★ Stihl Fingers	p. 199	Chainsaw
	☐ ★ ★ Drier Adhesive To The...	p. 183	Amazonia		☐ ★ ★ ★ Passage	p. 230	View East
	☐ ★ ★ To Crest In Violent ...	p. 225	Slumbersome		☐ ★ ★ ★ Empty Martyr...	p. 237	View West
	☐ ★ Semi-Suite	p. 177	Semi-Wall		☐ ★ ★ ★ Mr. Big	p. 193	Actual Cave
5.11b	☐ ★ ★ ★ ★ Crescendo Of The...	p. 213	Lost Resort	5.12b	☐ ★ ★ Bikini Girls With Turbo Drills	p. 191	Actual Cave
	☐ ★ ★ ★ Green Buddha	p. 220	Alpinia		☐ ★ ★ Cyanide	p. 193	Actual Cave
	☐ ★ ★ Stemming Out Beyond The	p. 225	Slumbersome	5.12c	☐ ★ ★ ★ And Empty It Remains	p. 237	View West
5.11c	☐ ★ ★ ★ ★ Giant	p. 193	Actual Cave	5.12d	☐ ★ Positive Vibrations	p. 193	Actual Cave
	☐ ★ ★ ★ ★ The Validity Of ...	p. 225	Slumbersome		☐ ★ Spartacus	p. 193	Actual Cave
	☐ ★ ★ ★ ★ Ataxicrack	p. 235	View West	5.13a	☐ ★ ★ Acid Rock	p. 193	Actual Cave
	☐ ★ ★ ★ My Evil Plan	p. 199	Chainsaw		☐ ★ ★ ★ Crawling From The...	p. 214	Lost Resort
	☐ ★ ★ ★ Give Your Shelf To Me	p. 213	Lost Resort				
	☐ ★ ★ ★ 100% Beef	p. 191	Actual Cave				
	☐ ★ ★ ★ Imbibing Knowledge...	p. 225	Slumbersome				
	☐ ★ ★ Semi-Automatic	p. 176	Semi-Wall				

Additional Area Information

Facilities

The available facilities at Exit-38 are part of the Ollalie State Park (www.parks.wa.gov) which borders the road after you take Exit-38 from I-90. They include a day-time only picnic area, toilets, and a public telephone. There is also a year-round toilet at the Mt Washingotn trail head.

Being a State Park has its advantages. One of the most useful is the availability of numerous Porta-Potties, i.e., Honey Buckets, Restrooms, Toilets, Plastic Crapper, Johnny on the Spot, Outhouses, Water Closets, Bathrooms, and Meditation Temples. There is one at the western side (by We Did Rock) and eastern side (by Hall Creek Rock). Never has an overly nervous climber had it so good. Note: The park removes the toilets in the fall and returns them again in the spring.

Since North Bend is so close, most out-of-town climbers crash at one of the inexpensive North Bend motels or just surprise a friend in Seattle since it's only a 30 minute drive from North Bend.

Camping

Camping in the Snoqualmie valley is really hit-or-miss. If it's a week day and not close to a holiday, then you can probably find a relatively quiet camp spot. If it's a warm and sunny holiday weekend then you'll most likely be spending the night in your car. The camp grounds are normally only open from early May to mid-October.

The closest State owned camping area (water, toilets, and no showers) is Tinkham campground. It is 4 miles further East on Interstate 90 at Exit 42. To reach it, take east bound Exit 42 and turn right at the top of the off ramp. Take the next left onto a dirt road and follow it for 1.5 miles. The campground turnoff will be on your left. There is a $7 per day camping fee. It's open from May 16th to Sept 15th.

Check www.parks.wa.gov for more information on camping in the area.

Additional Area Information

Weather

Exit 38 is usually too cold and wet during the winter, but in the spring and summer it's ideal for climbing given the temperature averages a comfortable 65- 70 degrees Fahrenheit.

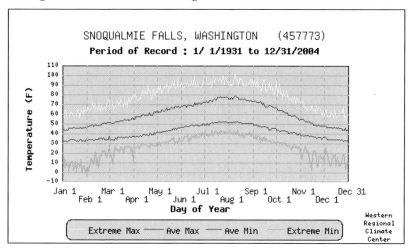

Getting to the top of a route and still being able to feel your hands is one thing but if the rock is wet, well, that's a bit more difficult. The graph below shows the average monthly rainfall for the Seattle area in a one year period i.e. June through September are the best months.

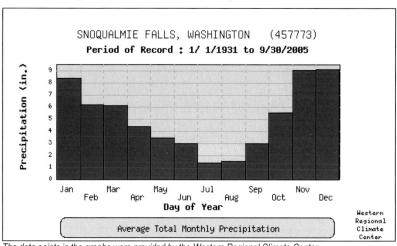

The data points in the graphs were provided by the Western Regional Climate Center.

Acknowledgements

There are many people and organizations that provide valuable services and support for Exit-38. Some notable ones include:

- **ACCESS FUND**: http://www.accessfund.org

- **WASHINGTON CLIMBERS COALITION**: http://www.washingtonclimbers.org/

- **WASHINTON TRAILS ASSOCIATION**: http://www.wta.org/

- **SEATTLE MOUNTAIN RESCUE**: http://www.smr001.net/

- **OLLALIE AND IRON HORSE PARK RANGERS**: http://www.parks.wa.gov/

- **FRIENDS OF THE TRAILS**: http://friendsofthetrail.org/

- **DEPARTMENT OF NATURAL RESOURCES**: http://www.wa.gov/dnr/

- **US NATIONAL FOREST SERVICE**: http://www.fs.fed.us/r6/welcome.shtml

Sport Climbing wouldn't be possible without the endless dedication by people who develop the climbing routes. These people have taken their own time, and money, to generously create routes at the Exit 38 area. Without their years of effort, sport climbing in the North Bend area wouldn't exist. They include Leland Windham, Bryan Burdo, Curtis "Lucky" Gibson, Mike Orr, Jeff Forister, Carrie Akerstrom, Keith Wentz, Dave Wolfe, Sarah Lenard, Mike Orr, CP Little, Mack Johnson, Dale Fleshman, Tucker Carlton, Jean Pierre Banville, Laura Orr, Ed Sewell, Adam Zeldt, Eric Ellis, Steve Martin, Matt Stanley, Dave Gunstone, Ethan Schwart, Brandon Kern, Drew Fletcher, Dave Perkins, and Lisa Lathe. Check www.northbendrock.com/routes/dev for more route development and First Ascent (FA) information.

Thanks to all the people who graciously allowed me to take photos of them; Wayne Miller, Jamie Harold, Danielle Giordano, Angela Harold, Joe and Taylor Levar, Marissa and Dan Young, Dave Argento and Mellisa Haltuch, the Luchtel family (Marcus, Natalie, David, and Debbi), Collen and Meg Meyers, and Chris Harrot.

Special thanks to Drew Fletcher and Dave Perkins for a summer of hard work developing the Neverland area, reviewing the book, replacing stolen hangers, working on trails, countless belays, and always having time for a cold one. Also, Jenn Carter for allowing me to fix her car in exchange for some fine editing work.

Finally, I would like to personally thank all the people who kept me focused on the book by telling me that a job and money aren't really that important.